HIGHBALLS
FOR BREAKFAST

The very best of

P.G. WODEHOUSE

on the joys of a good stiff drink

COMPILED AND EDITED BY

Richard T. Kelly

arrow books

1 3 5 7 9 10 8 6 4 2

Arrow Books
20 Vauxhall Bridge Road
London SW1V 2SA

Arrow Books is part of the Penguin Random House
group of companies whose addresses can be found at
global.penguinrandomhouse.com.

Penguin
Random House
UK

First published by Hutchinson in 2016
First published in paperback by Arrow Books in 2018

www.penguin.co.uk

A CIP catalogue record for this book is available
from the British Library.

ISBN 9781787462045

Typeset in 11.23/15.80 pt AdobeCaslonPro by Jouve (UK), Milton Keynes
Printed and bound in Great Britain by Clays Ltd, Elcograf S.p.A.

Penguin Random House is committed to a
sustainable future for our business, our readers
and our planet. This book is made from Forest
Stewardship Council® certified paper.

CONTENTS

INTRODUCTION

By Richard T. Kelly

'There are moments when one needs a drink.
Are there moments, indeed, when one doesn't?'

Such are the thoughts of movie actor Mervyn Potter in P.G. Wodehouse's 1952 novel *Barmy in Wonderland*. But Potter is only one of many in Wodehouse's gallery of great comic characters whose habit it is to 'restore the tissues with a spot of alcohol'. Such restoration, though, can lead a Wodehouse hero into a few edgy escapades if they don't know when to stop. To wit: Mervyn Potter's remarks above are addressed to a hotelier whose bungalow he has burned to the ground, Mervyn's excuse being that he had got himself rather 'pie-eyed' and in 'the party spirit'.

That spirit is very much the presiding one of the book you have before you: a collection by one of the funniest writers who ever wrote, on one of the greatest subjects known to man or woman. No one had a better understanding than Wodehouse of alcohol's capacity for inducing or provoking lively behaviour; or of how to render its comic effect on a page. In this volume you will find all the very best bits in Wodehouse that involve getting outside a stiff drink, and getting in and out of all sorts of scrapes as a result.

Wodehouse – known as 'Plum' to his loved ones and legions of admirers – enjoyed a long and happy life (from 1881 to 1975) and a remarkably rich longevity as an author: his first novel was published in 1902, his last in 1974. 1915 alone saw the first appearances in print of his most beloved creations: Jeeves and Wooster (in a short story called 'Extricating Young Gussie') and the world of Blandings Castle (in the novel *Something Fresh*).

It's a little less well known that Wodehouse, though born in Guildford and schooled at Dulwich College, spent a substantial part of his life in the USA. As the late critic Christopher Hitchens once ventured, 'However much people like to yoke [Wodehouse] with the phrase "quintessentially English", it was on American soil that he did much if not most of his best work.'

There is, however, no need to pick allegiances or favourites here. When Wodehouse wrote about drinking, as on everything else, he did so with equal aplomb whichever side of the Atlantic he settled upon. He had a deep and loving appreciation both of the affable English country pub and the boisterous Manhattan barroom, and he could see their respective pleasures and distinctions when it came to the serving of the 'life-restoring fluid'.

There is sometimes a problem for readers in respect of the

great authors we associate with fine writing about alcohol – F. Scott Fitzgerald, say, or John Cheever – in that quite a few of said writers were alcoholics, and the flooded misery of that condition became wincingly clear whenever they wrote about booze. Wodehouse, though, flies breezily free of all that. For starters we must distinguish between Wodehouse's actual drinking habits and those of his fictional creations.

Though he coined dozens of brilliant euphemisms for the state of inebriation, Wodehouse himself could never have maintained his stunning and lifelong productivity had he spent very much time nursing a sore head. Rather, he kept to regular habits. He and his wife Ethel (they married in 1914) were by no means teetotal but nor were they known for over-indulgence. Wodehouse biographer Robert McCrum notes that in his latter decades he treated himself to just a single 'evening cocktail' around 6pm (albeit a 'lethal' martini).

When it came to the work, though – to his imaginative world that was uniquely his – Wodehouse wrote very much as if happiness could be found in a bottle: that the cure for most mental and emotional ailments lies in a tall, cold glass of something refreshing. He's a tonic in that way. His characters are interested in all the varieties of booze – cocktails, champagne, port, whisky, brandy, the humble pint of beer, even the fearsome *poteen* stilled from potatoes.

Wodehouse was very good on drinking to get up one's nerve, or drinking to drown a sorrow, or wanting a drink badly but just not getting served. He's exceptionally good on hangovers and the diverse types thereof, but equally good on hangover cures (*cf.* the legendary pick-me-ups Jeeves prepares for Bertie Wooster). And when a character suffers a hangover in Wodehouse it's usually a prelude to something really nice happening to them – as it so often isn't in life, alas.

In short, no one writes quite so fondly and well as Wodehouse of 'the magic bottle', 'wine, the healer', 'the cup that clears today of past regrets and future fears'. As such we trust you will find that this book brings good cheer – and makes you also, perhaps, a bit thirsty.

I
EUPHEMISMS!
(AS ONE MIGHT SAY . . .)

'Intoxicated? The word did not express it by a mile.
He was oiled, boiled, fried, plastered, whiffled,
sozzled, and blotto.'

FROM WODEHOUSE'S 'THE STORY OF WILLIAM',
IN *MEET MR MULLINER* (1927)

One might not rate it the absolute highest writerly distinction to be very good at euphemisms for being drunk. Coming up with these is, after all, a sort of national sport, or art-form, and a lot of us seem to have our favoured adjectives for the job. The point, though – as Wodehouse knew well – is that we do seem to need an awful lot of them, possibly because so much can happen to a person and a situation after drink has been taken. There are many degrees of incapacity and levels of merriment or dishevelment. Naturally, Wodehouse was not the inventor of every single term with which he is associated; nonetheless his powers of novelty in this department are truly remarkable.

Of course, certain euphemisms arise from the very British ten-dency toward politeness and discreetness – not wishing to say of a thing that it is quite what it is. In The Inimitable Jeeves *(1923) Bertie Wooster finds his Aunt Agatha insisting that he accompany 'poor Uncle George to Harrogate for a few weeks' as he 'has had a severe shock' and needs to 'take the waters'.*

'What shock has he had?' I asked.

'Between ourselves,' said Aunt Agatha, lowering her voice in an impressive manner, 'I incline to think that the whole affair was the outcome of an over-excited imagination. You are one of the family, Bertie, and I can speak freely to you. You know as well as I do that your poor Uncle George has for many years not been a – he has – er – developed a habit of – how shall I put it?'

'Shifting it a bit?'

'I beg your pardon?'

'Mopping up the stuff to some extent?'

'I dislike your way of putting it exceedingly, but I must confess that he has not been, perhaps, as temperate as he should . . .'

Sometimes the level of consumption and the gravity of a situation mean that one can't always be as delicate as Aunt Agatha. For instance, at a late stage of Joy in the Morning *(1947) Boko Fittleworth has to give an alarming report to Bertie Wooster of his Uncle Percy, a.k.a Lord Worplesdon – and to do so with no nicety:*

'A wholly unforeseen situation has arisen. Old Worplesdon has gone to earth in the bar and is lowering the stuff by the pailful.'

Equally blunt in his assessment is Sir Aylmer Bostock in Uncle Dynamite *(1948), while complaining to his wife that their young nephew Bill Oakshott has turned up at the family's country seat in an inebriated state.*

'Do you know what that young hound did? Didn't get out at Ashenden Oakshott. Remained skulking in the train, went on to Bishop's Ickenham and turned up hours later in a car belonging to Lord Ickenham, stewed to the gills.'

In fact Bill Oakshott is not so stewed as his uncle imagines. But quite often in Wodehouse such accusations are levelled entirely accurately, and the sport arises from how the accused will choose to respond to the charge. In The Girl in Blue *(1970) country squire Crispin Scrope, greatly vexed by the loss of a valuable miniature painting, looks for help from his rather unreliable butler Chippendale only to find the man ensconced in the library, feet up and seeming to be notably refreshed.*

'Chippendale,' he said, 'you've been drinking.'
So manifestly true was this charge that the blush of shame would have mantled the cheek of a more sensitive man, but Chippendale acknowledged it with no change of colour . . .

'The merest spot, chum,' he said, 'the merest spot. I looked in at the Goose and Gander for a few quick ones . . .'

'How,' [Crispin] asked, 'are you going to find that miniature when you're as tight as an owl?'

Chippendale weighed the question, and it amused him a good deal. He had to laugh like an entertained hyaena before he could reply. He knew that after those quick ones he was at the top of his form. Recovering his gravity, he admitted that he was perhaps a mite polluted, but ridiculed the suggestion that he was as tight as an owl.

'Just keyed up, chum. In the circumstances, if I may use the expression, a couple of snifters were unavoidable . . .'

Barmy in Wonderland's *Mervyn Potter is another who maintains that his alcohol intake is a largely 'unavoidable' thing. Hotel employee Barmy Fotheringay-Phipps is often forced to suffer the consequences of Mervyn's overindulgence; at times blameless Barmy even finds himself maligned by Mervyn as the cause of it all.*

'Mervyn, you're blotto!'

A bitter hiccough escaped Mervyn Potter.

'And who wouldn't be after an evening with Fotheringay-Phipps?' he demanded. 'There's a wild Indian for you. He turned up at my apartment and intimidated me from the start. He's one of those fellows who get very ugly when sozzled, and I could see from his manner as he muscled in that he was fried to the gills.'

Putting such slender excuses aside, an outbreak of good news remains the best pretext for a good stiff drinking binge. Thus Edmund Biffen 'Biff' Christopher in Frozen Assets *(1964), who heads out on the town after learning that he will receive his godfather's substantial legacy, and stumbles in on his pal Jerry quite a few merry hours later. (Additionally, if we can say that certain great writers make particular words 'their own', this was certainly the case with Wodehouse and 'uvula' – the proper name for the little bit of skin tissue that dangles from one's soft palate.)*

'Hi Jerry,' [Biff] said.

He spoke so thickly and was weaving so noticeably in his walk that Jerry was able to form an instant diagnosis.

'Biff, you're blotto!'

'And why not?' said Biff warmly. He made a movement to seat himself, missed the chair by some inches and continued his remarks from the floor. 'You don't become a millionaire every day, do you? And it's a poor heart that never rejoices, isn't it? You can take it from me, Jerry o' man, that if a fellow raised from rags to riches at the breakfast table isn't tanked to the uvula by nightfall, it simply means he hasn't been trying . . .'

There are times, though, when the keen drinker, challenged on his drunkenness, must put up his paws and admit, however euphemistically, that it's a fair cop. In The Mating Season *(1949) Bertie Wooster gets into such a condition, having with his friend Esmond Haddock knocked back most of a decanter of port then climbed onto the dining-room table to deliver a song or two, only to be surprised by the sudden appearance of his aunt, Dame Daphne Winkworth. Later, mulling over Dame Daphne's frosty reaction, Bertie has to wonder if he has not, perhaps, given the wrong impression.*

I am not saying that this woman's words, with their underlying suggestion that I was fried to the tonsils, had not wounded me. It was all too plainly her opinion that, if let loose in drawing-rooms, I would immediately proceed to create an atmosphere reminiscent of a waterfront saloon when the Fleet is in. But the Woosters are essentially fair-minded, and I did not blame her for holding these views. I could quite see that when you come into a dining-room and find a guest leaping about with a decanter in his hand, singing Hallo, hallo, hallo, hallo, a-hunting we will go, my lads, a-hunting we will go, you are pretty well bound to fall into a certain train of thought ... [T]he port which I had swigged perhaps a little too freely in Esmond Haddock's society was of a fine old vintage and full of body. It now struck me that it must have had even more authority than I had supposed and that Dame Daphne Winkworth had been perfectly correct in assuming that I was scrooched.

2

'THE THIRST OF WHICH HE WAS DYING'

Most of us will know times in life when the thrill of a thing lies in the chase more than the capture: when having the urge proves a more exciting experience than that urge's final fulfilment. For instance, is there a drink so quenching that it can truly measure up to a thirst on which one has been working steadily for hours? Wodehouse certainly had some thoughts on this matter.

In Laughing Gas *(1936) Reginald ('Reggie') Swithin, third Earl of Havershot, is assigned by his Aunt Clara to travel to Hollywood and bring home her son Eggy before he gets himself hitched to some gold digger. And yet, as a result of a mishap of cosmic proportions while under anaesthetic at the dentist's, Reggie exchanges bodies with child movie star Joey Cooley. Not the least of Reggie's problems in this reduced 12-year-old physical state is how he is to deal with the regular urges of his grown-up inner self, such as this one:*

It was suddenly borne in upon me that I was dying of thirst. What with the warmth of the day and the fact that I had so recently been taking vigorous outdoor exercise, the epiglottis seemed to have become composed of sandpaper. Already I was gasping painfully like a stranded fish, and it seemed to me that if I didn't climb outside something moist in about half a jiffy, I should expire in dreadful agonies.

And this thought had scarcely flitted into my mind when I noticed that all the materials for a modest binge were hospitably laid out on a table in the corner. There was the good old decanter, the jolly old syphon, the merry bucket of ice, and, in brief, the whole bag of tricks. They seemed to be beckoning to me, and I tottered across like a camel making for an oasis and started mixing.

Of course, I ought to have realized that, while this urge to have a couple of quick ones was Lord Havershot's, the capacity for absorbing the stuff would be little Joey Cooley's; but at the moment, I confess, it didn't occur to me. I filled a flagon and drained it at a gulp.

It didn't seem to taste as good as I had expected, so I had another to see if I really liked it.

The sandpaper epiglottis suffered by Reggie has its twin in Uncle Dynamite's *Pongo Twistleton. While staying with his prospective father-in-law at Ashenden Manor, Pongo finds himself in a state of high anxiety around midnight one night — mainly because he is aware that come 1 a.m. his Uncle Fred (a.k.a. Lord Ickenham) will launch an attempt to break in and burgle the house.*

As Pongo paced the floor, from time to time quivering all over like a Brazilian explorer with a touch of malaria, he was still in faultless evening dress, for the idea of going to bed on this night of fear had not even occurred to him . . . And it is probable that mental distress would have unstrung him completely, but for the fact that in addition to suffering agony of the soul he was also in the process of dying of thirst, and this seemed to act on the counter-irritation principle.

The thirst of which he was dying was one of those lively young thirsts which seems to start at the soles of the feet and get worse all the way up. Growing in intensity ever since his arrival at the house, it had reached its peak at eleven o'clock tonight, when Jane, the parlour-maid, had brought the bedtime decanter and syphon into the drawing-room. He was no weakling, but having to sit there watching his host, his uncle and Bill Oakshott getting theirs like so many stags at eve – he himself, in deference to his known prejudice against alcoholic liquor, having been served with barley water – had tested his iron control almost beyond endurance.

For some minutes he continued to pace the floor, cursing the mad impulse which had led him to tell Hermione that he never touched the stuff and sketching out in his mind the series of long, cool ones with which, if he ever got out of here alive, he would correct this thirst of his. And then, as he reached the end of the carpet and was about to turn and pace back again, he stopped abruptly with one foot in the air, looking so like *The Soul's Awakening* that a seasoned art critic would have been deceived. Two chimes had just sounded from the church tower, and it was as if they had been the voice of a kindly friend whispering in his ear.

'Aren't you,' they seemed to say, 'overlooking the fact that that decanter is still in the drawing-room? One merely throws this out as a suggestion.' And he saw that here was the solution of what had appeared to be an impasse. His guardian angel, for he presumed it was his guardian angel, had pointed out the way.

Hats off to the good old guardian angel, was Pongo's attitude.

A minute later he was in the corridor. Three minutes later he was in the drawing-room. Three and a quarter minutes later he was pouring with trembling fingers what promised to be the snifter of a lifetime. And four minutes later, reclining in an armchair with his feet on a small table, he had begun to experience that joy, than which there is none purer, which comes to the unwilling abstainer who has at last succeeded in assembling the materials . . .

Wodehouse could also conjure the special frustration and melancholy of one who is thirsty for a drink and yet made to endure the purgatory of a wait to get served. Freddie Rooke, a supporting figure in Jill the Reckless *(1920), has some profound thoughts on this line while slumped unhappily in an armchair at the Drones Club, waiting for his friend Algy Martyn to show up so that festivities may start.*

Doctors, laying down the law in their usual confident way, tell us that the vitality of the human body is at its lowest at two o'clock in the morning: and that it is then, as a consequence, that the mind is least able to contemplate the present with equanimity, the future with fortitude, and the past without regret. Every thinking man, however, knows that this is not so. The true zero hour, desolate, gloom-ridden, and spectre-haunted, occurs immediately before dinner while we are waiting for that cocktail. It is then that, stripped for a brief moment of our armour of complacency and self-esteem, we see ourselves as we are – frightful chumps in a world where nothing goes right; a grey world in which, hoping to click, we merely get the raspberry; where, animated by the best intentions, we nevertheless succeed in perpetrating the scaliest bloomers and landing our loved ones neck-deep in the gumbo . . .

It would have been bad enough in any case, for Algy Martyn was late as usual and it always gave Freddie the pip to have to wait for dinner: but what made it worse was the fact that the Drones was not one of Freddie's clubs and so, until the blighter Algy arrived, it was impossible for him to get his cocktail. There he sat, surrounded by happy, laughing young men, each grasping a glass of the good old mixture-as-before, absolutely unable to connect. Some of them, casual acquaintances, had nodded to him, waved, and gone on lowering the juice – a spectacle which made Freddie feel much as the wounded soldier would have felt if Sir Philip Sidney, instead of offering him the cup of water, had placed it to his own lips and drained it with a careless 'Cheerio!' No wonder Freddie experienced the sort of abysmal soul-sadness which afflicts one of Tolstoi's Russian peasants when, after putting in a heavy day's work strangling his father, beating his wife, and dropping the baby into the city reservoir, he turns to the cupboard, only to find the vodka-bottle empty.

Waiting to be served at the bar, of course, one may occasionally run the risk of being told that this wait will be infinite – for the reason that one has 'had too many already'. Wodehouse evokes this special thirsty hell in Cocktail Time *(1958), the sufferer being Cosmo Wisdom, patron of the Beetle and Wedge pub, whose stern landlord is Rupert Morrison.*

It sometimes happens at the Beetle and Wedge that a customer, demanding home-brew and licking his lips at the prospect of getting it, is informed by the voice of doom, speaking in the person of Rupert Morrison, that he has already had enough and cannot be served. On such occasions the customer has the feeling that the great globe itself has faded, leaving not a wrack behind, and that, as in the case of bad men interrupted in their activities by the United States Marines, all is darkness, disillusionment and despair. Such a feeling came to Cosmo Wisdom now ...

The dry-lipped condition of thirsting for a drink might not strike everyone as a source of fine poetry. Yet in Greek mythology Hippocrene was a spring on Mount Helicon, and its waters, blessed by the Muses, had the power to inspire mortals to verse. The myth of Hippocrene certainly made a great impression on the poet Keats – and on Wodehouse, in turn, for in Pigs Have Wings *(1952) he gave the humble pigman George Cyril Wellbeloved a thirst worthy of that illustrious name.*

Although nobody who had met him would have been likely to get George Cyril Wellbeloved confused with the poet Keats, it was extraordinary on what similar lines the two men's minds worked. 'Oh, for a beaker full of the warm South, full of the true, the blushful Hippocrene!' sang Keats, licking his lips, and 'Oh, for a mug of beer with, if possible, a spot of gin in it!' sighed George Cyril Wellbeloved, licking his.

3

STIFFISH, WITH SODA

'A diet of large whiskies and small sodas, persisted in through the whole of a long afternoon and evening and augmented by an occasional neat brandy, is a thing which cuts, as it were, both ways.'

BIG MONEY (1931)

Bertie Wooster counts himself as a careful drinker. And so when in The Code of the Woosters *(1938) he is summoned to see his Aunt Dahlia and given an ear-bashing for his alleged intemperance ('Don't you ever stop drinking? How about when you are asleep?') Bertie defends himself with dignity.*

'You wrong me, relative. Except at times of special revelry, I am exceedingly moderate in my potations. A brace of cocktails, a glass of wine at dinner and possibly a liqueur with the coffee – that is Bertram Wooster . . .'

That is a fib, of course. Leaving aside the generous definition of what constitutes 'special revelry', the careful reader knew since the 1916 story 'Jeeves and the Unbidden Guest' that Jeeves brings Bertie a 'nightly whisky-and-soda'. That classic combination of any-spirit-and-soda that Americans dubbed a 'highball' is a recurrent tipple in Wodehouse and especially dear to Bertie, who – as we learn in The Inimitable Jeeves – has exacting requirements for the measures involved.

'I say, Jeeves,' I said.

'Sir?'

'Mix me a stiffish brandy and soda.'

'Yes, sir.'

'Stiffish, Jeeves. Not too much soda, but splash the brandy about a bit.'

Another Wodehouse character impartial as to what spirit goes into his highball is Eggy Mannering. In Laughing Gas he unaccountably lands an assignment as an elocution teacher for a Hollywood studio, and when asked to expound on his preferred methods of speech therapy he resorts to the thing he knows and likes best.

'I'll tell you,' he said. 'Methods differ. There are various schools of thought. Some have one system, some another. I, personally, like to begin by taking a good stiff Scotch and soda—'

'What!'

'Or, better, two Scotch and sodas. This keys up the brain and puts one in the vein to instruct. So if you have Scotch in the house—'

'We do not.'

'Then make it rye,' said Eggy, full of resource.

The stiffness is the thing, though, if the mix is to work its magic, and not just for Bertie and Eggy. Hugo Carmody in the Blandings Castle novel Summer Lightning *(1929) also turns out to have an exact preference in the matter, revealed to the reader when he rejoins his friend Sue Brown in a hotel lobby having stepped out to take a ticklish phone call from his fiancée, Millicent Threepwood.*

'Hugo,'[Sue] cried, as that lucky young man returned and dropped into the chair at her side. 'Hugo, listen!'

'I say,' said Hugo.

'I've suddenly thought . . .'

'I say,' said Hugo.

'Do listen!'

'I say,' said Hugo, 'that was Millicent on the 'phone.'

'Was it? How nice. Listen, Hugo . . .'

'Speaking from Blandings.'

'Yes. But . . .'

'And she has broken off the engagement!'

'What!'

'Broken off the bally engagement,' repeated Hugo. He signalled urgently to a passing waiter. 'Get me a brandy-and-soda, will you?' he said. His face was pale and set. 'A stiffish brandy-and-soda, please.'

'Brandy-and-soda, sir?'

'Yes,' said Hugo. 'Stiffish.'

But if for poor Hugo the highball is only a means of drowning sorrow, it is the very stuff of life and vigour for 'Squiffy' Bixby, a.k.a. Lord Tidmouth, in Doctor Sally *(1932). A lovelorn chap named Bill Bannister is the witness when Squiffy, his eye 'fixed purposefully on the decanter on the table', approaches it 'with a stealthy rapidity, like a panther' then fills a glass, whereupon he feels fit for conversation.*

'They say,' continued Lord Tidmouth earnestly, 'that strong drink biteth like a serpent and – if I remember correctly – stingeth like a jolly old adder. Well, all I have to say is – let it! That's what I say, Bill – let it! It's what it's there for. Excuse me for a minute, old man, while I mix myself a stiffish serpent-and-soda ...'

4

THE COCKTAILS
OF A LIFETIME

Jeeves, perpetually extricating Bertie from scrapes, is forced to resort to extreme measures at the end of Jeeves in the Offing: *namely to spread a falsehood that the young master is in fact a mentally disturbed kleptomaniac not responsible for his actions. Bertie, in no way grateful – in fact, outraged – asks Jeeves how he is supposed to survive this indignity while sitting at a dinner table with people who believe him to be off his rocker.*

'My advice, sir, would be to fortify yourself for the ordeal.'

'How?'

'There are always cocktails, sir. Shall I pour you another?'

'You should.'

In other words, there are times when a highball won't suffice – when only the special concoction of a cocktail can hit the spot. This distinction is keenly explored in 'The Passing of Ambrose' from Mr

Mulliner Speaking (1929). Ambrose Wiffin, having been lumbered with the chore of minding two beastly children for an afternoon, allows himself to imagine the reward he will give himself once his martyrdom is done.

Ambrose, greatly restored, turned to sketching out in his mind the details of the drink which his man, under his own personal supervision, should mix for him immediately upon his return. As to this he was quite clear. Many fellows in his position – practically, you might say, saved at last from worse than death – would make it a stiff whisky-and-soda. But Ambrose, though he had no prejudice against whisky-and-soda, felt otherwise. It must be a cocktail. The cocktail of a lifetime. A cocktail that would ring down the ages, in which gin blended smoothly with Italian vermouth and the spot of old brandy nestled like a trusting child against the dash of absinthe . . .

In Wodehouse people are very often coming over all misty-eyed about the merits of particular cocktail recipes. In Summer Lightning *even Galahad Threepwood, a fairly confirmed highball man, is found reminiscing fondly to his brother Clarence's butler Beach about the pleasures of the mint-julep:*

'. . . Have you ever tasted a mint-julep, Beach?'

'Not to my recollection, sir.'

'Oh, you'd remember all right if you had. Insidious things. They creep up on you like a baby sister and slide their little hands into yours and the next thing you know the Judge is telling you to pay the clerk of the court fifty dollars ...'

The mint julep, of course, is a celebrated and simple construction: a couple of jiggers of bourbon whiskey, some mint leaves, a little sugar, a little water, and a handful of cracked ice. In Uncle Fred in the Springtime *Lord Ickenham – albeit masquerading as the eminent brain specialist Sir Roderick Glossop, identity fraud being common practice at Blandings Castle – gives the highly anxious Horace Pendlebury-Davenport a much more complicated prescription for the medicine he needs to get down him.*

'My dear boy ... Do we by any chance know a beverage called May Queen? Its full name is 'Tomorrow'll be of all the year the maddest, merriest day, for I'm to be Queen of the May, mother, I'm to be Queen of the May.' A clumsy title, generally shortened for purposes of ordinary conversation. Its foundation is any good, dry champagne, to which is added liqueur brandy, armagnac, kummel, yellow chartreuse and old stout, to taste. It is a good many years since I tried it myself, but I can thoroughly recommend it to alleviate the deepest despondency [...]'

On the subject of mixtures, Jeeves is unsurprisingly expert and a connoisseur. In Jeeves and the Feudal Spirit *Bertie sings the praises of a preparation of Jeeves's that he calls the 'special'.*

While I'm dressing, will you be mixing me a strengthening cocktail?'

'Certainly, sir. A martini or one of my specials?'

'The latter.'

It was in quite fairly tense mood that I dried and clothed the person, and while it would perhaps be too much to say that as I entered the sitting-room some quarter of an hour later I was a-twitter, I was unquestionably conscious of a certain jumpiness. When Jeeves came in with the shaker, I dived at it like a seal going after a slice of fish and drained a quick one, scarcely pausing to say 'Skin off your nose'.

The effect was magical. That apprehensive feeling left me, to be succeeded by a quiet sense of power. I cannot put it better than by saying that, as the fire coursed through my veins, Wooster the timid fawn became in a flash Wooster the man of iron will, ready for anything. What Jeeves inserts in these specials of his I have never ascertained, but their morale-building force is extraordinary. They wake the sleeping tiger in a chap. Well, to give you some idea, I remember once after a single one of them striking the table with clenched fist and telling my Aunt Agatha to stop talking rot. And I'm not sure it wasn't 'bally rot'.

The close reader will have spotted that Bertie, as keen and eloquent as he is on the effects of the Jeeves special, has no real inkling of, or interest in, the ingredients Jeeves has used to mix it. In short, he is content to be a customer, and to let the creative magic happen out of sight. In 'The Rummy Affair of Old Biffy', a tale in the collection Carry On Jeeves *(1925), Bertie is similarly pleased to be relieved by another's ingenuity, having been coerced into trudging round the stalls of the 'British Empire Exhibition' at Wembley, in the company of his pal Biffy and Biffy's prospective father-in-law – the afore-mentioned Sir Roderick Glossop.*

Well, you know, I have never been much of a lad for exhibitions. The citizenry in the mass always rather puts me off, and after I have been shuffling along with the multitude for a quarter of an hour or so I feel as if I were walking on hot bricks.

By the time we had tottered out of the Gold Coast village and were working towards the Palace of Machinery, everything pointed to my shortly executing a quiet sneak in the direction of that rather jolly Planters' Bar in the West Indian section. Sir Roderick had whizzed us past this at a high rate of speed, it touching no chord in him; but I had been able to observe that there was a sprightly sportsman behind the counter mixing things out of bottles and stirring them up with a stick in long glasses that seemed to have ice in them, and the urge came upon me to see more of this man. I was about to drop away from the main body and become a straggler, when something pawed at my coat-sleeve. It was Biffy, and he had the air of one who has had about sufficient.

There are certain moments in life when words are not

needed. I looked at Biffy, Biffy looked at me. A perfect understanding linked our two souls.

'?'

'!'

Three minutes later we had joined the Planters.

I have never been in the West Indies, but I am in a position to state that in certain of the fundamentals of life they are streets ahead of our European civilisation. The man behind the counter, as kindly a bloke as I ever wish to meet, seemed to guess our requirements the moment we hove in view. Scarcely had our elbows touched the wood before he was leaping to and fro, bringing down a new bottle with each leap. A planter, apparently, does not consider he has had a drink unless it contains at least seven ingredients, and I'm not saying, mind you, that he isn't right. The man behind the bar told us the things were called Green Swizzles; and, if ever I marry and have a son, Green Swizzle Wooster is the name that will go down on the register, in memory of the day his father's life was saved at Wembley.

It's the names of cocktails, rather than the naming of their parts, that quite often leave the strongest mark on Wodehouse characters. In 'Extricating Young Gussie', Jeeves and Bertie travel to New York, Bertie on a mission for his Aunt Agatha to bring home her son Augustus ('Gussie') before he gets hitched to a girl with whom he is smitten and who is – of all things – a performer on the vaudeville stage. Pitching up in Manhattan and finding Gussie not at his hotel, Bertie has no particular Plan B.

I admit I was hard hit. There I was alone in a strange city and no signs of Gussie . . . However, some instinct took me through a door at the back of the lobby, and I found myself in a large room with an enormous picture stretching across the whole of one wall, and under the picture a counter, and behind the counter divers chappies in white, serving drinks. They have barmen, don't you know, in New York, not barmaids. Rum idea!

I put myself unreservedly into the hands of one of the white chappies. He was a friendly soul, and I told him the whole state of affairs. I asked him what he thought would meet the case.

He said that in a situation of that sort he usually prescribed a 'lightning whizzer', an invention of his own. He said this was what rabbits trained on when they were matched against grizzly bears, and there was only one instance on record of the bear having lasted three rounds. So I tried a couple, and, by Jove! the man was perfectly right.

As I drained the second a great load seemed to fall from my heart, and I went out in quite a braced way to have a look at the city . . .

Bertie's light-heartedness, alas, cannot last. He runs into Gussie, right enough, but only for the fellow to tell him a grim tale: Gussie has fallen in love, and for the sake of that love has further formed the ambition of a career for himself in vaudeville.

I steadied myself against the wall. The effects of the restoratives supplied by my pal at the hotel bar were beginning to work off, and I felt a little weak. Through a sort of mist I seemed to have a vision of Aunt Agatha hearing that the head of the Mannering-Phippses was about to appear on the vaudeville stage . . . So what Aunt Agatha would say – beyond saying that it was all my fault – when she learned the horrid news, it was beyond me to imagine.

'Come back to the hotel, Gussie,' I said. 'There's a sportsman there who mixes things he calls 'lightning whizzers'. Something tells me I need one now . . .'

5
DUTCH COURAGE

Another favourite situation in Wodehouse is the need for a stiff one not simply to 'restore the tissues' but to embolden oneself for an onerous assignment. Often, that task is related to the vexing business of romance. A veritable masterclass on how this can be done is offered in A Damsel in Distress *(1919) by Reggie Byng, who is, indeed, somewhat boastful on the subject given that the friend with whom he shares his wisdom – George Bevan – is suffering the agonies of unrequited love and finds Reggie's success rather a torture.*

(Note, too, that a key comic component of this passage is that Reggie draws on a truly bumper yield of euphemisms for drunkenness – almost as though Wodehouse had set himself a challenge of cramming in a particular quota.)

'By the way, I forgot to ask. How is your little affair coming along? Everything going all right?'

'In a way,' said George. He was not equal to confiding his troubles to Reggie.

'Of course, your trouble isn't like mine was. What I mean is, Maud loves you, and all that, and all you've got to think out is a scheme for laying the jolly old family a stymie. It's a pity – almost – that yours isn't a case of having to win the girl, like me; because by Jove, laddie,' said Reggie with solemn emphasis, 'I could help you there. I've got the thing down fine. I've got the infallible dope.'

George smiled bleakly.

'You have? You're a useful fellow to have around. I wish you would tell me what it is.'

'But you don't need it.'

'No, of course not. I was forgetting.'

Reggie looked at his watch.

'We ought to be shifting in a quarter of an hour or so. I don't want to be late ... Well, as I was saying, I've got the dope. A week ago I was just one of the mugs – didn't know a thing about it – but now! Gaze on me, laddie! You see before you old Colonel Romeo, the Man who Knows! It all started on the night of the ball. There was the dickens of a big ball, you know, to celebrate old Boots' coming-of-age – to which, poor devil, he contributed nothing but the sunshine of his smile, never having learned to dance. On that occasion a most rummy and extraordinary thing happened. I got pickled to the eyebrows!' He laughed happily. 'I don't mean that that was a unique occurrence and so forth, because, when I was a bachelor, it was rather a habit of mine to get a trifle submerged every now and again on occasions of decent mirth and festivity. But the rummy thing that night was that I showed it. Up till then, I've been told by experts,

I was a chappie in whom it was absolutely impossible to detect the symptoms. You might get a bit suspicious if you found I couldn't move, but you could never be certain. On the night of the ball, however, I suppose I had been filling the radiator a trifle too enthusiastically. You see, I had deliberately tried to shove myself more or less below the surface in order to get enough nerve to propose to Alice. I don't know what your experience has been, but mine is that proposing's a thing that simply isn't within the scope of a man who isn't moderately woozled. I've often wondered how marriages ever occur in the dry States of America. Well, as I was saying, on the night of the ball a most rummy thing happened. I thought one of the waiters was you?'

He paused impressively to allow this startling statement to sink in.

'And was he?' said George.

'Absolutely not! That was the rummy part of it. He looked as like you as your twin brother.'

'I haven't a twin brother.'

'No, I know what you mean, but what I mean to say is he looked just like your twin brother would have looked if you had had a twin brother. Well, I had a word or two with this chappie, and after a brief conversation it was borne in upon me that I was up to the gills. Alice was with me at the time, and noticed it too. Now you'd have thought that that would have put a girl off a fellow, and all that. But no. Nobody could have been more sympathetic. And she has confided to me since that it was seeing me in my oiled condition that really turned the scale. What I mean is, she made up her mind to save me from myself. You know how some girls are. Angels absolutely! Always on the look out to pluck brands from the burning, and what not. You may take it from me that the good seed was definitely sown that night ...'

6

'A WOMAN IS ONLY A WOMAN . . .'

As most of us discover, for better or worse, a stiff drink can also function as a solace in cases of heartache: an anaesthetic to the pain caused by a romantic rejection.

In his 1886 poem 'The Betrothed' young Rudyard Kipling writes in the voice of a man pressed by his fiancée to choose between her affections and his love of cigars. 'A woman is only a woman,' this narrator concludes, 'but a good cigar is a smoke.' Wodehouse evidently knew Kipling's work; and while his characters might prefer to get the girl, they do tend, should things fall apart, to accept the consolation of the bottle.

In Pigs Have Wings Sir Gregory Parsloe is presented as an abstemious sort who even bans his pigman George Cyril Wellbeloved from the simple pleasure of an after-work beer while pointing to himself as a model ('Look at me. I never touch the stuff'). Pride comes before a fall, though, and when Sir Gregory suffers something of a romantic reversal, the surprise causes him to realise that self-denial brings suffering of its own, and that he has been unfairly neglecting an old friend in liquid form.

Sir Gregory was mildly fond of Gloria Salt, and had been on the whole rather attracted by the idea of marrying her, but it had not taken him long to see that there was a lot to be said in favour of the celibate life. What was enabling him to bear his loss with such fortitude was the realisation that, now that she had gone and broken off the dashed engagement, there was no longer any need for that bally dieting and exercising nonsense. Once more he was the master of his fate, the captain of his soul, and if he felt like widening his waist-line, could jolly well widen it, and no kick coming from any quarter. For days he had been yearning for beer with an almost Wellbelovedian intensity, and he was now in a position to yield to the craving. A tankard stood beside him at this very moment, and in the manner in which he raised it to his lips there was something gay and swashbuckling. A woman is only a woman, he seemed to be saying, but a frothing pint is a drink.

And so, even more so, are two frothing pints.

In Hot Water *(1932), Packy Franklyn, a wealthy Yale man, is engaged to Lady Beatrice Bracken, a highly principled English-woman to whom Packy pledges that he will cause no embarrassment by his actions. And yet, as a result of trying to do a young woman a good turn and the regrettable confusion arising from same, Packy gets very much on Lady Beatrice's long side and is told by her, in essence, that 'Those wedding-bells shall not ring out'. Shot to the heart, he considers his next move.*

Statisticians who have gone carefully into the figures – the name of Schertfeger of Berlin is one that springs to the mind – inform us that of young men who have just received a negative answer to a proposal of marriage (and with these must, of course, be grouped those whose engagements have been broken off) 6.08 per cent clench their hands and stare silently before them, 12.02 take the next train to the Rocky Mountains and shoot grizzlies, while 11.07 sit down at their desks and become modern novelists.

The first impulse of the remainder – and these, it is will be seen, constitute a large majority – is to nip off round the corner and got a good, stiff drink.

Into this class Packy fell. The imperious urge to put something cold and stimulating inside him swept over him within ten seconds of his perusal of the opening sentences of Beatrice's letter. Two minutes later, he was in the cocktail bar entreating the kindly Gustave to come to aid of the party. And it was while the latter was reaching for bottles and doing musical things with ice that he observed Senator Opal bearing down on him . . .

He had no wish to chat with the Senator, and only the intense desire to get outside a Gustave special immediately held him where he stood . . .

Packy's Gustave Special had arrived. He drained it without replying, and asked for another. The kindly Gustave, who could read faces, had foreseen the repeat order. He filled it instantaneously, and Packy snatched at the glass like a frightened child reaching for its mother's hand.

Pride of place among Wodehouse's tales of this type, and worthy of lengthy extraction, is 'The Story of William' from Meet Mr Mulliner *(1927) – Mulliner being an agreeable chap given to telling tales of his family to regular habitués of and visitors to the Angler's Rest pub.*

This particular tale concerns how Mulliner's Uncle William once managed against all odds to win the heart of a woman called Myrtle Banks during the San Francisco Earthquake of 1906. Things had looked bad, for William had a rival in Desmond Franklyn, a venturesome outdoorsman who had duelled with sharks and rhinoceroses, and whose proposal of marriage Myrtle duly accepted. Singing in jealousy's flame William hotly advised her to throw over this 'perisher'. Whereupon, as Mr Mulliner tells it . . .

The girl rose in a marked manner.

'I do not require your advice, Mr. Mulliner,' she said, coldly. 'And I have not changed my mind.'

Instantly William Mulliner was all contrition. There is a certain stage in the progress of a man's love when he feels like curling up in a ball and making little bleating noises if the object of his affections so much as looks squiggle-eyed at him; and this stage my Uncle William had reached. He followed her as she paced proudly away through the hotel lobby, and stammered incoherent apologies. But Myrtle Banks was adamant.

'Leave me, Mr. Mulliner,' she said, pointing at the revolving door that led into the street. 'You have maligned a better man than yourself, and I wish to have nothing more to do with you. Go!'

William went, as directed. And so great was the confusion of his mind that he got stuck in the revolving door and had gone round in it no fewer than eleven times before the hall-porter came to extricate him.

'I would have removed you from the machinery earlier, sir,' said the hall-porter deferentially, having deposited him safely in the street, 'but my bet with my mate in there called for ten laps. I waited till you had completed eleven so that there should be no argument.'

William looked at him dazedly.

'Hall-porter,' he said.

'Sir?'

'Tell me, hall-porter,' said William, 'suppose the only girl you have ever loved had gone and got engaged to another, what would you do?'

The hall-porter considered.

'Let me get this right,' he said. 'The proposition is, if I have followed you correctly, what would I do supposing the Jane on whom I had always looked as a steady mamma had handed me the old skimmer and told me to take all the air I needed because she had gotten another sweetie?'

'Precisely.'

'Your question is easily answered,' said the hall-porter.

'I would go around the corner and get me a nice stiff drink at Mike's Place.'

'A drink?'

'Yes, sir. A nice stiff one.'

'At – where did you say?'

'Mike's Place, sir. Just round the corner. You can't miss it.'

William thanked him and walked away. The man's words had started a new, and in many ways interesting, train of thought. A drink? And a nice stiff one? There might be something in it.

William Mulliner had never tasted alcohol in his life. He had promised his late mother that he would not do so until he was either twenty-one or forty-one – he could never remember which. He was at present twenty-nine; but wishing to be on the safe side in case he had got his figures wrong, he had remained a teetotaller. But now, as he walked listlessly along the street towards the corner, it seemed to him that his mother in the special circumstances could not reasonably object if he took a slight snort. He raised his eyes to heaven, as though to ask her if a couple of quick ones might not be permitted; and he fancied that a faint, far-off voice whispered, 'Go to it!'

And at this moment he found himself standing outside a brightly-lighted saloon.

For an instant he hesitated. Then, as a twinge of anguish in the region of his broken heart reminded him of the necessity for immediate remedies, he pushed open the swing doors and went in.

The principal feature of the cheerful, brightly-lit room in which he found himself was a long counter, at which were standing a number of the citizenry, each with an elbow on the woodwork and a foot upon the neat brass rail which ran below. Behind the counter appeared the upper section of one of the most benevolent and kindly-looking men that William had ever seen. He had a large smooth face, and he wore a white coat, and he eyed William, as he advanced, with a sort of reverent joy.

'Is this Mike's Place?' asked William.

'Yes, sir,' replied the white-coated man.

'Are you Mike?'

'No, sir. But I am his representative, and have full authority to act on his behalf. What can I have the pleasure of doing for you?'

The man's whole attitude made him seem so like a large-hearted elder brother that William felt no diffidence about confiding in him. He placed an elbow on the counter and a foot on the rail, and spoke with a sob in his voice.

'Suppose the only girl you had ever loved had gone and got engaged to another, what in your view would best meet the case?'

The gentlemanly bar-tender pondered for some moments.

'Well,' he replied at length, 'I advance it, you understand, as a purely personal opinion, and I shall not be in the least offended if you decide not to act upon it; but my suggestion – for what it is worth – is that you try a Dynamite Dew-Drop.'

One of the crowd that had gathered sympathetically round shook his head. He was a charming man with a black eye, who had shaved on the preceding Thursday.

'Much better give him a Dreamland Special.'

A second man, in a sweater and a cloth cap, had yet another theory.

'You can't beat an Undertaker's Joy.'

They were all so perfectly delightful and appeared to have his interests so un-selfishly at heart that William could not bring himself to choose between them. He solved the problem in diplomatic fashion by playing no favourites and ordering all three of the beverages recommended.

The effect was instantaneous and gratifying. As he drained the first glass, it seemed to him that a torchlight procession, of whose existence he had hitherto not been aware, had begun to march down his throat and explore the recesses of his stomach.

The second glass, though slightly too heavily charged with molten lava, was extremely palatable. It helped the torchlight procession along by adding to it a brass band of singular power and sweetness of tone. And with the third somebody began to touch off fireworks inside his head.

William felt better – not only spiritually but physically. He seemed to himself to be a bigger, finer man, and the loss of Myrtle Banks had somehow in a flash lost nearly all its importance. After all, as he said to the man with the black eye, Myrtle Banks wasn't everybody.

'Now what do you recommend?' he asked the man with the sweater, having turned the last glass upside down.

The other mused, one forefinger thoughtfully pressed against the side of his face.

'Well, I'll tell you,' he said. 'When my brother Elmer lost his girl, he drank straight rye. Yes, sir. That's what he drank – straight rye. "I've lost my girl," he said, "and I'm going to drink straight rye." That's what he said. Yes, sir, straight rye.'

'And was your brother Elmer,' asked William, anxiously, 'a man whose example in your opinion should be followed? Was he a man you could trust?'

'He owned the biggest duck-farm in the southern half of Illinois.'

'That settles it,' said William. 'What was good enough for a duck who owned half Illinois is good enough for me. Oblige me,' he said to the gentlemanly bar-tender, 'by asking these gentlemen what they will have, and start pouring.'

The bar-tender obeyed, and William, having tried a

pint or two of the strange liquid just to see if he liked it, found that he did, and ordered some. He then began to move about among his new friends, patting one on the shoulder, slapping another affably on the back, and asking a third what his Christian name was.

'I want you all,' he said, climbing on to the counter so that his voice should carry better, 'to come and stay with me in England. Never in my life have I met men whose faces I liked so much. More like brothers than anything is the way I regard you. So just you pack up a few things and come along and put up at my little place for as long as you can manage. You particularly, my dear old chap,' he added, beaming at the man in the sweater.

'Thanks,' said the man with the sweater.

'What did you say?' said William.

'I said, "Thanks".'

William slowly removed his coat and rolled up his shirt-sleeves.

'I call you gentlemen to witness,' he said, quietly, 'that I have been grossly insulted by this gentleman who has just grossly insulted me. I am not a quarrelsome man, but if anybody wants a row they can have it. And when it comes to being cursed and sworn at by an ugly bounder in a sweater and a cloth cap, it is time to take steps.'

And with these spirited words William Mulliner sprang from the counter, grasped the other by the throat, and bit him sharply on the right ear. There was a confused interval, during which somebody attached himself to the collar of William's waistcoat and the seat of William's trousers, and then a sense of swift movement and rush of cool air.

William discovered that he was seated on the pavement outside the saloon. A hand emerged from the swing door and threw his hat out. And he was alone with the night and his meditations.

These were, as you may suppose, of a singularly bitter nature. Sorrow and disillusionment racked William Mulliner like a physical pain. That his friends inside there, in spite of the fact that he had been all sweetness and light and had not done a thing to them, should have thrown him out into the hard street was the saddest thing he had ever heard of; and for some minutes he sat there, weeping silently.

Presently he heaved himself to his feet and, placing one foot with infinite delicacy in front of the other, and then drawing the other one up and placing it with infinite delicacy in front of that, he began to walk back to his hotel.

At the comer he paused. There were some railings on his right. He clung to them and rested awhile.

The railings to which William Mulliner had attached himself belonged to a brownstone house of the kind that seems destined from the first moment of its building to receive guests, both resident and transient, at a moderate weekly rental. It was, in fact, as he would have discovered had he been clear-sighted enough to read the card over the door, Mrs. Beulah O' Brien's Theatrical Boarding-House ('A Home From Home – No Cheques Cashed – This Means You').

But William was not in the best of shape for reading cards. A sort of mist had obscured the world, and he was finding it difficult to keep his eyes open. And presently, his chin wedged into the railings, he fell into a dreamless sleep.

He was awakened by light flashing in his eyes; and, opening them, saw that a window opposite where he was standing had become brightly illuminated. His slumbers had cleared his vision; and he was able to observe that the room into which he was looking was a dining-room. The long table was set for the evening meal; and to William, as he gazed, the sight of that cosy apartment, with the gaslight falling on the knives and forks and spoons, seemed the most pathetic and poignant that he had ever beheld.

A mood of the most extreme sentimentality now had him in its grip. The thought that he would never own a little home like that racked him from stem to stern with an almost unbearable torment. What, argued William, clinging to the railings and crying weakly, could compare, when you came right down to it, with a little home? A man with a little home is all right, whereas a man without a little home is just a bit of flotsam on the ocean of life. If Myrtle Banks had only consented to marry him, he would have had a little home. But she had refused to marry him, so he would never have a little home. What Myrtle Banks wanted, felt William, was a good swift clout on the side of the head.

The thought pleased him. He was feeling physically perfect again now, and seemed to have shaken off completely the slight indisposition from which he had been suffering. His legs had lost their tendency to act independently of the rest of his body. His head felt clearer, and he had a sense of overwhelming strength. If ever, in short, there was a moment when he could administer that clout on the side of the head to Myrtle Banks as it should be administered, that moment was now.

He was on the point of moving off to find her and teach her what it meant to stop a man like himself from having a little home, when someone entered the room into which he was looking, and he paused to make further inspection.

The new arrival was a coloured maid-servant. She staggered to the head of the table beneath the weight of a large tureen containing, so William suspected, hash. A moment later a stout woman with bright golden hair came in and sat down opposite the tureen.

The instinct to watch other people eat is one of the most deeply implanted in the human bosom, and William lingered, intent. There was, he told himself, no need to hurry. He knew which was Myrtle's room in the hotel. It was just across the corridor from his own. He could pop in any time, during the night, and give her that clout. Meanwhile, he wanted to watch these people eat hash.

And then the door opened again, and there filed into the room a little procession.

And William, clutching the railings, watched it with bulging eyes.

The procession was headed by an elderly man in a check suit with a carnation in his buttonhole. He was about three feet six in height, though the military jauntiness with which he carried himself made him seem fully three feet seven. He was followed by a younger man who wore spectacles and whose height was perhaps three feet four.

And behind these two came, in single file, six others, scaling down by degrees until, bringing up the rear of the procession, there entered a rather stout man in tweeds and bedroom slippers who could not have measured more than two feet eight.

They took their places at the table. Hash was distributed to all. And the man in tweeds, having inspected his plate with obvious relish, removed his slippers and, picking up his knife and fork with his toes, fell to with a keen appetite.

William Mulliner uttered a soft moan, and tottered away.

It was a black moment for my Uncle William. Only an instant before he had been congratulating himself on having shaken off the effects of his first indulgence in alcohol after an abstinence of twenty-nine years; but now he perceived that he was still intoxicated.

Intoxicated? The word did not express it by a mile. He was oiled, boiled, fried, plastered, whiffled, sozzled, and blotto. Only by the exercise of the most consummate caution and address could he hope to get back to his hotel and reach his bedroom without causing an open scandal.

Of course, if his walk that night had taken him a few yards farther down the street than the door of Mike's Place, he would have seen that there was a very simple explanation of the spectacle which he had just witnessed. A walk so extended would have brought him to the San Francisco Palace of Varieties, outside which large posters proclaimed the exclusive engagement for two weeks of

MURPHY'S MIDGETS.

Bigger and Better than Ever.

But of the existence of these posters he was not aware; and it is not too much to say that the iron entered into William Mulliner's soul.

That his legs should have become temporarily unscrewed at the joints was a phenomenon which he had been able to bear with fortitude. That his head should be feeling as if a good many bees had decided to use it as a hive was unpleasant, but not unbearably so. But that his brain should have gone off its castors and be causing him to see visions was the end of all things [...]

Moodily he made his way back to his hotel. In a corner of the Palm Room he saw Myrtle Banks deep in conversation with Franklyn, but all desire to give her a clout on the side of the head had now left him. With his chin sunk on his breast, he entered the elevator and was carried up to his room.

Here as rapidly as his quivering fingers would permit, he undressed; and, climbing into the bed as it came round for the second time, lay for a space with wide-open eyes. He had been too shaken to switch his light off, and the rays of the lamp shone on the handsome ceiling which undulated above him. He gave himself up to thought once more.

No doubt, he felt, thinking it over now, his mother had had some very urgent reason for withholding him from alcoholic drink. She must have known of some family secret, sedulously guarded from his infant ears – some dark tale of a fatal Mulliner taint.

'William must never learn of this!' she had probably said when they told her the old legend of how every Mulliner for centuries back had died a maniac, victim at last to the fatal fluid. And to-night, despite her gentle care, he had found out for himself.

He saw now that this derangement of his eyesight was only the first step in the gradual dissolution which was the Mulliner Curse. Soon his sense of hearing would go, then his sense of touch.

He sat up in bed. It seemed to him that, as he gazed

at the ceiling, a considerable section of it had parted from the parent body and fallen with a crash to the floor.

William Mulliner stared dumbly. He knew, of course, that it was an illusion. But what a perfect illusion! If he had not had the special knowledge which he possessed, he would have stated without fear of contradiction that there was a gap six feet wide above him and a mass of dust and plaster on the carpet below.

And even as his eyes deceived him, so did his ears. He seemed to be conscious of a babel of screams and shouts. The corridor, he could have sworn, was full of flying feet.

The world appeared to be all bangs and crashes and thuds. A cold fear gripped at William's heart. His sense of hearing was playing tricks with him already.

His whole being recoiled from making the final experiment, but he forced himself out of bed. He reached a finger towards the nearest heap of plaster and drew it back with a groan. Yes, it was as he feared, his sense of touch had gone wrong too. That heap of plaster, though purely a figment of his disordered brain, had felt solid.

So there it was. One little moderately festive evening at Mike's Place, and the Curse of the Mulliners had got him. Within an hour of absorbing the first drink of his life, it had deprived him of his sight, his hearing, and his sense of touch. Quick service, felt William Mulliner.

As he climbed back into bed, it appeared to him that two of the walls fell out. He shut his eyes, and presently sleep, which has been well called Tired Nature's Sweet Restorer, brought oblivion. His last waking thought was that he imagined he had heard another wall go.

William Mulliner was a sound sleeper, and it was many hours before consciousness returned to him. When he awoke, he looked about him in astonishment. The haunting horror of the night had passed; and now, though conscious of a rather severe headache, he knew that he was seeing things as they were.

And yet it seemed odd to think that what he beheld was not the remains of some nightmare. Not only was the world slightly yellow and a bit blurred about the edges, but it had changed in its very essentials overnight. Where eight hours before there had been a wall, only an open space appeared, with bright sunlight streaming through it. The ceiling was on the floor, and almost the only thing remaining of what had been an expensive bedroom in a first-class hotel was the bed. Very strange, he thought, and very irregular.

A voice broke in upon his meditations.

'Why, Mr. Mulliner!'

William turned, and being, like all the Mulliners, the soul of modesty, dived abruptly beneath the bed-clothes. For the voice was the voice of Myrtle Banks. And she was in his room!

'Mr. Mulliner!'

William poked his head out cautiously. And then he perceived that the proprieties had not been outraged as he had imagined.

Miss Banks was not in his room, but in the corridor. The intervening wall had disappeared. Shaken, but relieved, he sat up in bed, the sheet drawn round his shoulders.

'You don't mean to say you're still in bed?' gasped the girl.

'Why, is it awfully late?' said William.

'Did you actually stay up here all through it?'

'Through what?'

'The earthquake.'

'What earthquake?'

'The earthquake last night.'

'Oh, that earthquake?' said William, carelessly. 'I did notice some sort of an earthquake. I remember seeing the ceiling come down and saying to myself, "I shouldn't wonder if that wasn't an earthquake." And then the walls fell out, and I said, "Yes, I believe it is an earthquake." And then I turned over and went to sleep.'

Myrtle Banks was staring at him with eyes that reminded him partly of twin stars and partly of a snail's.

'You must be the bravest man in the world!'

William gave a curt laugh.

'Oh, well,' he said, 'I may not spend my whole life persecuting unfortunate sharks with pocket-knives, but I find I generally manage to keep my head fairly well in a crisis. We Mulliners are like that. We do not say much, but we have the right stuff in us.'

He clutched his head. A sharp spasm had reminded him how much of the right stuff he had in him at that moment.

'My hero!' breathed the girl, almost inaudibly.

7

GOD'S OWN ENGLISH COUNTRY PUB

As we have seen, Green Swizzles, Lightning Whizzers and the like are all well and good in their time and place; but a frothing pint is also a drink to be reckoned with, and a pub is quite the best place to reckon it. Wodehouse had a special place in his heart and a special gift for evoking the sort of rural village pub where a soul can sit in peace and wile away hours.

Consider this lovely idyll from the story 'Anselm Gets His Chance' in the 1940 collection Eggs, Beans and Crumpets:

The Summer Sunday was drawing to a close. Twilight had fallen on the little garden of the Angler's Rest, and the air was fragrant with the sweet scent of jasmine and tobacco plant. Stars were peeping out. Blackbirds sang drowsily in the shrubberies. Bats wheeled through the shadows, and a gentle breeze played fitfully among the hollyhocks. It was, in short, as a customer who had looked in for a gin and tonic rather happily put it, a nice evening.

The Angler's Rest is, of course, the public house frequented by racon-teur Mr Mulliner; the place where he politely listens into local conversations and chips in with stories from his familial recol-lections that contain some useful lesson or other. Mulliner's usual drink is a hot Scotch and lemon, from which he takes measured sips. His pub companions don't go by regular monikers but are characterised by their own regular tipple: thus 'Draught Stout', 'Double-Whisky-and-Splash', 'Small Bass', 'Gin-and-Ginger-Ale', 'Lemonade and Angustura', etc. It is a settled world, and Mulliner notes as much in Mr Mulliner Speaking *(1929).*

I have heard it said that the cosy peace which envelops the bar-parlour of the Angler's Rest has a tendency to promote in the regular customers a certain callousness and indifference to human suffering. I fear there is something in the charge. We who have made the place our retreat sit sheltered in a backwater far removed from the rushing stream of Life. We may be dimly aware that out in the world there are hearts that ache and bleed: but we order another gin and ginger and forget about them. Tragedy, to us, has come to mean merely the occa-sional flatness of a bottle of beer.

*If the Angler's Rest is its own universe, Wodehouse was able to create something more in the manner of a pub-crawl itinerary in imagin-ing the layout of Market Blandings, the nearest town to Lord Emsworth's Blandings Castle. (*Pigs Have Wings *offers a partial roll-call of the town's hostelries: 'the Emsworth Arms, the Wheatsheaf,* *the Waggoner's Rest, the Beetle and Wedge, the Stitch in Time, the Jolly Cricketers . . .') The Emsworth Arms, though, is the primus inter pares of Market Blandings pubs, known for 'the excellence of its beer and the charm of the shady garden'. It is introduced to readers in* Something Fresh, *the first of the Blandings novels, through the eyes of Rupert ('The Efficient') Baxter, austere secretary to Lord Emsworth.*

Having bought his tobacco and observed the life and thought of the town for half an hour . . . [Baxter] made his way to the Emsworth Arms, the most respectable of the eleven inns which the citizens of Market Blandings contrived in some miraculous way to support. In most English country towns, if the public houses do not actually outnumber the inhabitants, they all do an excellent trade. It is only when they are two to one that hard times hit them and set the innkeepers blaming the Government.

Aside from the riverside situation, the generous garden and comfortable armchairs, the Emsworth Arms is also celebrated, of course, for the drinks it purveys, pre-eminently a very special beer. In Uncle Fred in the Springtime *(1939) young Ricky Gilpin – disappointed in the pursuit of funds for a business venture by which he hoped to endear himself to the girl he adores – discovers that beer's restorative powers.*

Ricky had come to the private bar in search of relief for his bruised soul, and he could have made no wiser move.

Nothing can ever render the shattering of his hopes and the bringing of his dream castles to ruin about his ears really agreeable to a young man, but the beer purveyed by G. Ovens, proprietor of the Emsworth Arms, unquestionably does its best. The Ovens home-brewed is a liquid Pollyanna, for ever pointing out the bright side and indicating silver linings. It slips its little hand in yours, and whispers 'Cheer up!' If King Lear had had a tankard of it handy, we should have had far less of that 'Blow, winds, and crack your cheeks!' stuff.

On Ricky it acted like magic ... Money, the beer pointed out, was not everything. 'Look at it this way,' it argued. 'It's absurd to say there aren't a hundred ways by which a smart and enterprising young fellow can get enough money to marry on. The essential thing about this marrying business is not money, but the girl. If the girl's all right, everything's all right. [...] And something is sure to turn up.'

This wondrous beer's ability to lift spirits is further illustrated in Service with a Smile *(1962). The villainous Duke of Dunstable, who takes a dim view of Lord Emsworth, conspires to steal the man's prize pig and sell this creature to Lord Tilbury (enlisting Emsworth's latest secretary Lavender Briggs into the scheme.) Meeting with Tilbury in the pub to seal the deal, Dunstable is reminded he feels no fondness towards a man he knew at school as 'Stinker Pyke' – and yet, gradually, a certain something serves to warm his feelings.*

[The Duke] was now fairly full of the Emsworth Arms beer, and, as everybody who has tried it knows, there is something about the home-brewed beer purveyed by G. Ovens, landlord of the Emsworth Arms, that has a mellowing effect. What G. Ovens put into it is a secret between him and his Maker, but it acts like magic on the most reticent. With a pint of this elixir sloshing about inside him, it seemed to the Duke that it would be churlish not to share his happiness with a sympathetic crony.

'Just put one over on a blasted female,' he said.

The promising conversation, though, soon dwindles, as Dunstable begins to realise the truth of the adage that 'one is not enough'.

There is just this one thing more to be said about G. Ovens' home-brewed beer. If you want to preserve that mellow fondness for all mankind which it imparts, you have to go on drinking it. The Duke, having had only a single pint, was unable to retain the feeling that Lord Tilbury was a staunch friend from whom he could have no secrets. He was conscious of a vivid dislike for him, and couldn't imagine why a gracious sovereign had bestowed a barony on a man like that . . .

The Emsworth Arms is not the only Blandings hostelry to boast of a famous homebrew. There is also the Beetle and Wedge (landlord: Rupert Morrison.) It's there that Albert Peasemarch, butler to Sir

Raymond Bastable, is asked by Lord Ickenham ('Uncle Fred') to hold a certain secret document in safekeeping – a task at which Albert quails initially, since Ickenham makes the favour sound like a full-blown espionage adventure. (It's not, of course.) Still, having had one beer contemplatively, Peasemarch decides to consider Ickenham's request over a second.

'Another of the same, please, Mr M,' he said, and Rupert Morrison once more became the human St Bernard dog.

The results were instantaneous – indeed, magical would scarcely be too strong a word. Until now, the chronicler has merely hinted at the dynamic properties of the Beetle and Wedge home-brew. The time has come to pay it the marked tribute it deserves. It touched the spot. It had everything. It ran like fire through Albert Peasemarch's veins and made a new man of him. The careworn, timorous Albert Peasemarch ceased to be, and in his place there sat an Albert Peasemarch filled to the brim with the spirit of adventure. A man of regular habits, he would normally have shrunk from playing a stellar role in an E. Phillips Oppenheim story, as he appeared to be doing now, but with the home-brew lapping up against his back teeth he liked it. 'Bring on your ruddy spies!' about summed up his attitude.

8

OLD DEVILS

'I don't know if you've ever met my Uncle George.
He's a festive old egg who wanders from club to club
continually having a couple with other festive old
eggs. When he heaves in sight, waiters brace
themselves up and the wine-steward toys with his
corkscrew. It was my Uncle George who discovered
that alcohol was a food well in advance of
modern medical thought.'

THE INIMITABLE JEEVES

Wodehouse attained a ripe age in life by dint of looking after
himself fairly carefully – calisthenics in the morning, a regular diet,
and just that 'lethal martini' in the evening with the sun well
over the yardarm. In his writings, though, he created more than a
few recurring characters – such as Bertie Wooster's Uncle George –
who thrived into their later years by perpetual indulgence. Chief
among these is Lord Emsworth's younger brother, The Hon. Galahad
Threepwood. In Summer Lightning (1929), his appearance is
introduced like so:

The Hon. Galahad Threepwood, in his fifty-seventh year, was a dapper little gentleman on whose grey but still thickly-covered head the weight of a consistently misspent life rested lightly.

Gally's views on a good diet are expressed vigorously in Heavy Weather *(1933):*

'No healthy person really needs food. If people would only stick to drinking, doctors would go out of business.'

His admirers do marvel at what he subsists upon, as in Full Moon *(1947):*

'He had discovered the prime grand secret of eternal youth – to keep the decanter circulating and never to go to bed before four in the morning.'

The best evocation of Gally's charm and endurance is in the aforementioned Summer Lightning, *this extract expressing his devotion to drink, his refusal of all substitutes, and also his fondness for anecdotes, which he is forever pledging to collect in a memoir.*

A thoroughly misspent life had left the Hon. Galahad Threepwood, contrary to the most elementary justice, in what appeared to be perfect, even exuberantly perfect physical condition. How a man who ought to have had the liver of the century could look and behave as he did was a constant mystery to his associates. His eye was not dimmed nor his natural force abated. And when, skipping blithely across the turf, he tripped over the spaniel, so graceful was the agility with which he recovered his balance that he did not spill a drop of the whisky and soda in his hand. He continued to bear the glass aloft like some brave banner beneath which he had often fought and won. Instead of the blot on the proud family, he might have been a teetotal acrobat.

Having disentangled himself from the spaniel and soothed the animal's wounded feelings by permitting it to sniff the whisky-and-soda, the Hon. Galahad produced a black-rimmed monocle, and, screwing it into his eye, surveyed the table with a frown of distaste.

'Tea?'

Millicent reached for a cup.

'Cream and sugar, Uncle Gally?'

He stopped her with a gesture of shocked loathing.

'You know I never drink tea. Too much respect for my inside. Don't tell me you are ruining your inside with that poison.'

'Sorry, Uncle Gally. I like it.'

'You be careful,' urged the Hon. Galahad, who was fond of his niece and did not like to see her falling into bad habits. 'You be very careful how you fool about with that stuff. Did I ever tell you about poor Buffy Struggles back in 'ninety-three? Some misguided person lured poor old Buffy into one of those temperance lectures illustrated with coloured slides, and he called on me next day ashen, poor old chap – ashen. "Gally," he said. "What would you say the procedure was when a fellow wants to buy tea? How would a fellow set about it?" "Tea?" I said. "What do you want tea for?" "To drink," said Buffy. "Pull yourself together, dear boy," I said. "You're talking wildly. You can't drink tea. Have a brandy and soda." "No more alcohol for me," said Buffy. "Look what it does to the common earthworm." "But you're not a common earthworm," I said, putting my finger on the flaw in his argument right away. "I dashed soon shall be if I go on drinking alcohol," said Buffy. Well, I begged him with tears in my eyes not to do anything rash, but I couldn't move him. He ordered in ten pounds of the muck and was dead inside the year.'

'Good heavens! Really?'

The Hon. Galahad nodded impressively.

'Dead as a door-nail. Got run over by a hansom cab, poor dear old chap, as he was crossing Piccadilly. You'll find the story in my book.'

'How's the book coming along?'

'Magnificently, my dear. Splendidly.'

9
PURITANS AND BORES

'I have never been able to understand what pleasure
men can find in spirituous liquors. Lemonade is so
much more refreshing. I drink nothing else myself.'

HERMIONE BRIMBLE, IN 'THE RIGHT APPROACH'
FROM *A FEW QUICK ONES*

Given the affection Wodehouse reserves for cheery serial tipplers, you
can well imagine the rough treatment he dishes out to characters
who make a terrific show of never touching a drop. A degree of moderation, at times, is commendable, perhaps – but someone who
abstains entirely simply cannot be serious.

Temperance is easily satirised – for instance, by Archibald Mulliner
in 'The Reverend Wooing of Archibald' from Mr Mulliner Speaking. There, attempting to win the affections of Aurelia Cammerleigh
through an act of impressing the girl's aunt, Archibald opts for a
demeanour of piety, dons 'a pair of horn-rimmed spectacles which
gave him something of the look of an earnest sheep', and in the aunt's
company contrives:

To say some rather caustic things about the practice, so prevalent among his contemporaries, of drinking cocktails. Life, said Archibald, toying with his teacup, was surely given to us for some better purpose than the destruction of our brains and digestions with alcohol.

But if Archibald is only feigning, Wodehouse knew that some people talk this sort of rot in deadly earnest. In A Damsel in Distress *Percy Wilbraham Marsh is subjected to a thorough dose of it from a rural curate, who mistakes Percy's hot temper and dishevelled appearance for that of 'a victim of the Demon Rum'.*

'You ought to be ashamed of yourself,' he said severely. 'Sad piece of human wreckage as you are, you speak like an educated man. Have you no self-respect? Do you never search your heart and shudder at the horrible degradation which you have brought on yourself by sheer weakness of will?'

He raised his voice. The subject of Temperance was one very near to the curate's heart. The vicar himself had complimented him only yesterday on the good his sermons against the drink evil were doing in the village, and the landlord of the Three Pigeons down the road had on several occasions spoken bitter things about blighters who came taking the living away from honest folks.

'It is easy enough to stop if you will but use a little

resolution. You say to yourself, 'Just one won't hurt me!' Perhaps not. But can you be content with just one? Ah! No, my man, there is no middle way for such as you. It must be all or nothing. Stop it now – *now*, while you still retain some semblance of humanity. Soon it will be too late! Kill that craving! Stifle it! Strangle it! Make up your mind now – *now*, that not another drop of the accursed stuff shall pass your lips . . .'

The curate paused. He perceived that enthusiasm was leading him away from the main issue. 'A little perseverance,' he concluded rapidly, 'and you will soon find that cocoa gives you exactly the same pleasure'. . .

Fatigue, pain and the annoyance of having to listen to this man's well-meant but ill-judged utterances had combined to induce in Percy a condition bordering on hysteria. He stamped his foot, and uttered a howl as the blister warned him with a sharp twinge that this sort of behaviour could not be permitted.

'Stop talking!' he bellowed. 'Stop talking like an idiot! . . .'

One figure in Wodehouse to whom sanctimony is quite alien is Stanley Featherstonehaugh Ukridge, an opportunistic schemer forever on the look-out for a smart way to line his pockets. In 'The Exit of Battling Billson' from the 1924 collection Ukridge, *narrator James 'Corky' Corcoran runs into our man in Llunindnno, Wales, and finds his old friend has taken to managing a prize-fighter named Wilberforce Billson. But Battling Billson, it transpires, is changing*

his pugilistic ways, having heard the good word from a revivalist
preacher. Corky establishes as much when he sees Billson emerge
from a pub, in the wake of great shouting and smashing of glass,
and proudly claim responsibility for the ruckus.

'I been doin' good,' said Mr Billson, virtuously.

'Doing good?'

'Spillin' their beers.'

'Whose beers?'

'All of their beers. I went in and there was a lot of
sinful fellers drinkin' beers. So I spilled 'em. All of 'em.
Walked around and spilled all of them beers, one after
the other. Not 'arf surprised them pore sinners wasn't,'
said Mr Billson, with what sounded to me not unlike a
worldly chuckle.

'I can readily imagine it.'

'Huh?'

'I say I bet they were.'

'R!' said Mr Billson. He frowned. 'Beer,' he proceeded with cold austerity, 'ain't right. Sinful, that's what
beer is. It stingeth like a serpent and biteth like a ruddy
adder.'

My mouth watered a little. Beer like that was what I
had been scouring the country for for years. I thought it
imprudent, however, to say so. For some reason which I
could not fathom, my companion, once as fond of his
half-pint as the next man, seemed to have conceived a
puritanical hostility to the beverage ...

Never was beer more puritanically reviled in modern times than in the USA following the infamous Volstead Act of 1919, which decreed the prohibition of manufacture and sale of alcoholic beverages. But for the next ten years Prohibition singularly failed to stop a great many Americans getting fabulously drunk, and it gave Wodehouse a backdrop for some of his best tales, in which he treated the temperance mob to a thoroughly mocking eye.

Laughing Gas (1936) was composed not long after Prohibition was abolished in 1933 – and Alcoholics Anonymous subsequently formed in Akron, Ohio. Eggy Mannering has gone to Hollywood and got engaged to Ann Bannister, but she disapproves of his drinking and has banned him from indulging. Dropping in on his friend Reggie one day, Eggy is abruptly required to play host when a second unexpected visitor calls – a young woman of a marked austerity, to whom Eggy is civil in the standard manner:

'. . . [M]ay I offer you a spot?'

'A what?'

'A snifter. I can recommend the Scotch.'

'Are you suggesting that I should drink liquor?'

'That's the idea.'

'Well, let me tell you, Mr Man,—'

'- erring.'

'Pardon?'

'The name is Mannering.'

'Oh? Well, let me tell you, Mr Mannering, that I don't drink liquor. I have come here collecting subscriptions for the Temple of the New Dawn.'

'The – what was that again?'

'Haven't you ever heard of the Temple of the New Dawn?'

'Not that I remember.'

'Haven't you ever heard of Sister Lora Luella Scott?'

'No. Who is she?'

'She is the woman who is leading California out of the swamp of alcohol.'

'Good God!' I could tell by Eggy's voice that he was interested. 'Is there a swamp of alcohol in these parts? What an amazing country America is. Talk about every modern convenience. Do you mean you can simply go there and lap?'

'I was speaking figuratively.'

'I knew there was a catch,' said Eggy, disappointed.

'Sister Lora Luella is converting California to true temperance.'

'How perfectly frightful.'

10
ON THE WAGON

In a letter to a friend of June 1930 Wodehouse described 'a terrific attack of neuritis' he had recently suffered, the remedy for which required him 'to knock off drink' for six weeks. '[T]eetotalism certainly makes one frightfully fit,' he observed ruefully. The cure, however, could not hold. 'Then I had to go to a party,' Wodehouse confessed, 'and I couldn't go through it without cocktails.' To be on the wagon, as they say, is a testing journey down a rocky path, and it is common enough that one will fall off.

Wodehouse does not deny that the thing can be done to an extent, albeit at a price. In Much Obliged, Jeeves (1971), the penultimate Jeeves & Wooster novel, Bertie goes to lunch with old pal Ginger Winship, prospective MP for Market Snodsbury ('standing in the Conservative interest'). But Bertie's hopes that said lunch will have a strong liquid component are set to be dashed.

Arriving at Barribault's, I found [Ginger] in the lobby where you have the pre-luncheon gargle before proceeding to the grillroom, and after the initial What-ho-ing and What-a-time-since-we-met-ing, inevitable when two vanished hands who haven't seen each other for ages re-establish contact, he asked me if I would like one for the tonsils.

'I won't join you,' he said. 'I'm not actually on the wagon, I have a little light wine at dinner now and then, but my fiancée wants me to stay off cocktails. She says they harden the arteries.'

If you are about to ask me if this didn't make me purse the lips a little bit, I can assure you that it did. It seemed to point to his having gone and got hitched up with a popsy totally lacking in the proper spirit [...]'

A more forlorn evocation of the drinkless condition comes in Barmy in Wonderland, *when perennial hellraiser Mervyn Potter is made to realise that his fiancée Hermione Brimble is not prepared to tolerate his riotous behaviour on the pop. Seeing the worst of it writ large on the man's face, Barmy Fotheringay-Phipps wonders exactly what Hermione has said to Potter.*

'Has she given you the raspberry?'

'If by that you mean is the engagement off, the answer is no. We are still affianced. But at what a cost! At what a cost, Phipps! The boss has issued an ultimatum. From now on spirituous liquor is not to pass my lips. One move on my part toward the sauce, and those wedding bells will not ring out. Dating from tonight, I am on the wagon.'

Mervyn Potter fell into a sombre silence, his thoughts on the grey future.

'I wonder, Phipps,' he said, 'if you have the slightest conception what it means to be on the wagon. I shall go through the world a haunted man. There will be joy and mirth in that world, but not in the heart of Mervyn Potter. Everywhere around me I shall hear the happy laughter of children as they dig into their Scotch highballs, but I shall not be able to join them. I shall feel like a thirsty leper ...'

Wodehouse does, however, show us one way to get on the wagon and stay on it, though it's not one that the temperance brigade would approve on point of rigour. Galahad Threepwood is the vehicle for it in Heavy Weather, *as he recalls to Lord Tilbury ('Stinker' Pyke) the tale of their mutual friend Major Wilfred 'Plug' Basham, 'a fellow who never knew where to stop', for which reason Gally was moved to subject him to a would-be improving lecture:*

'I pointed out that all the trouble was caused by his fatal practice of always ordering a quart where other men began with pints. He saw it, too. "I know, I know," he said. "I'm a darned fool. In fact, between you and me, Gally, I suppose I'm one of those fellows my father always warned me against. But the Bashams have always ordered quarts. It's an old Basham family custom." Then, the only way was, I said, to swear off altogether. He said he couldn't. A little something with his meals was an absolute necessity to him. So there I had to leave it. And then one day I met him again at a wedding reception at one of the hotels.'

'I . . .' said Lord Tilbury.

'A wedding reception,' proceeded the Hon. Galahad. 'And, by a curious coincidence, there was another wedding reception going on at the same hotel, and, oddly enough, their bride was some sort of connection of our bride. So pretty soon these two wedding parties began to mix and mingle, everybody happy and having a good time, and suddenly I felt something pluck at my elbow and there was old Plug, looking as white as a sheet. "Yes Plug?" I said, surprised. The poor, dear fellow uttered a hollow groan. "Gally, old man," he said, "lead me away, old chap. The end has come. The stuff has begun to get me. I have had only the merest sip of champagne, and yet I assure you I can distinctly see two brides."'

'I . . .' said Lord Tilbury.

'A shock to the poor fellow, as you can readily imagine. I could have set his mind at rest, of course, but I saw that this was providential. Just the sort of jolt he had been needing. I drew him into a corner and talked to him like a Dutch uncle. And this time he gave me his solemn word that from that day onward he would never touch another drop. "Can you do it, Plug?" I said. "Have you the strength, the will-power?" "Yes, Gally," he replied bravely, "I can. Why, dash it," he said, "I've got to. I can't go through the rest of my life seeing two of everything. Imagine! Two bookies you owe money to . . . Two process-servers . . . Two Stinker Pykes . . ." Yes, old man, in that grim moment he thought of you . . . And he went off with a set, resolute look about his jaw which it did me good to see.'

'I . . .' said Lord Tilbury.

'And about two weeks later I came on him in the Strand, and he was bubbling over with quiet happiness. "It's all right, Gally," he said, "it's all right, old lad. I've done it. I've won the battle." "Amazing, Plug," I said. "Brave chap! Splendid fellow! Was it a terrific strain?" His eyes lit up. "It was at first," he said. "In fact, it was so tough that I didn't think I should be able to stick it out. And then I discovered a teetotal drink that is not only palatable but positively appetising. Absinthe, they call it, and now I've got that I don't care if I never touch wine, spirits, or any other intoxicants again."'

II

THE BACK OF THE DRINKS CABINET

Strictly speaking, the title of this chapter is a phrase usually invoked to describe the type of bottle rashly bought as a souvenir of a holiday overseas, then left to gather dust where the more respectable spirits need not have to look at it. Still, it will serve us pretty well for this selection of extracts in which Wodehouse describes the downing of certain alcoholic beverages less regularly served within his body of work, but none the less dynamic in their effects upon the drinker.

In 'Success Story', a tale from Nothing Serious (1950), *Stanley Featherstonehaugh Ukridge has a bothersome encounter with an officious butler in a pantry, leaving him in need of perking up by whatever liquid means he can locate.*

He left me flat, departing without a backward glance, and I started hunting round for the port. There should be some, I felt, in this pantry. 'If butlers come, can port be far behind?' is always a pretty safe rule to go on.

I located it eventually in a cupboard, and took a stimulating swig. It was just what I had been needing. It has frequently happened that a good go in at the port at a critical moment has made all the difference to me as a thinking force. The stuff seems to act directly on the little grey cells, causing them to flex their muscles and chuck their chests out. A stiff whisky and soda sometimes has a similar effect, I have noticed, but port never fails.

It did not fail me now.

In the story called 'Fate' from Young Men in Spats *(1936) Freddie Widgeon finds himself in scrapes just because of his willingness to help out struggling ladies – a gallantry that nonetheless costs him points with his fiancée. One such attempted kindness leads to his sitting in the apartment of a young woman in a pink negligee, and accepting from her a glass of the kind of lethal one-pot spirit that the people of the Appalachian mountains called 'moonshine', and which the Irish know as 'poteen'.*

'Have a drink,' said the female.

This seemed to old Freddie by miles the best suggestion yet. He sank into a chair and let his tongue hang out. And presently a brimming glass stole into his hand, and he quaffed deeply.

'That's some stuff I brought away from home,' said the female.

'From where?' said Freddie.

'Home.'

'But this isn't your home?'

'Well, it is now. But I used to live in Utica. Mr. Silvers made this stuff. About the only good thing he ever did. Mr. Silvers, I mean.' [. . .]

He quaffed again. The foundation of the beverage manufactured by Mr. Silvers seemed to be neat vitriol, but, once you had got used to the top of your head going up and down like the lid of a kettle with boiling water in it, the effects were far from unpleasant. Mr. Silvers may not have had ideals, but he unquestionably knew what to do when you handed him a still and a potato.

Champagne, surely, is the drink of kings, not to be bracketed with the poor stuff made out of corn mash or root vegetables? The answer, as so often, is 'It depends' – and the price-tag on a bottle of bubbly is usually indicative of the quality of drinking experience in store. In 'Ukridge's Accident Syndicate' (from Ukridge, *1924) our eponymous hero is forced to wrestle with these considerations when he tries to form a cabal of friends in order to pull off an accident insurance scam. The friend chosen to take the fall and suffer the accident that will trigger a pay-out is Teddy Weeks, but in order to brace himself for his ordeal Teddy has a special request.*

'I'll tell you what I'll do,' he said, suddenly. 'It's no use asking me to put this thing through in cold blood. I simply can't do it. I haven't the nerve. But if you fellows will give me a dinner tonight with lots of champagne I think it will key me up to it.'

A heavy silence fell upon the room. Champagne! The word was like a knell.

'How on earth are we going to afford champagne?' said Victor Beamish.

'Well, there it is,' said Teddy Weeks. 'Take it or leave it.'

'Gentlemen,' said Ukridge, 'it would seem that the company requires more capital. How about it, old horses? Let's get together in a frank, business-like, cards-on-the-table spirit, and see what can be done. I can raise ten bob.'

'What!' cried the entire assembled company, amazed. 'How?

'I'll pawn a banjo.'

'You haven't got a banjo.'

'No, but George Tupper has, and I know where he keeps it.'

Started in this spirited way, the subscriptions came pouring in. I contributed a cigaratte-case, Bertram Fox thought his landlady would let him owe for another week, Robert Dunhill had an uncle in Kensington who, he fancied, if tactfully approached, would be good for a quid, and Victor Beamish said that if the advertisement-manager of the O-so-Eesi Piano-Player was churlish enough to refuse an advance of five shillings against future work he misjudged him sadly. Within a few minutes, in short, the Lightning Drive had produced the impressive total of two pounds six shillings, and we asked Teddy Weeks if he thought that he could get adequately keyed up within the limits of that sum.

THE BACK OF THE DRINKS CABINET

'I'll try,' said Teddy Weeks.

So, not unmindful of the fact that that excellent hostelry supplied champagne at eight shillings the quart bottle, we fixed the meeting for seven o' clock at Barolini's.

Considered as a social affair, Teddy Weeks's keying-up dinner was not a success. Almost from the start I think we all found it trying. It was not so much the fact that he was drinking deeply of Barolini's eight-shilling champagne while we, from lack of funds, were compelled to confine ourselves to meaner beverages; what really marred the pleasantness of the function was the extraordinary effect the stuff had on Teddy. What was actually in the champagne supplied to Barolini and purveyed by him to the public, such as were reckless enough to drink it, at eight shillings the bottle, remains a secret between its maker and his Maker; but three glasses of it were enough to convert Teddy Weeks from a mild and rather oily young man into a truculent swashbuckler.

He quarrelled with us all. With the soup he was tilting at Victor Beamish's theories of Art; the fish found him ridiculing Bertram Fox's views on the future of the motion-picture; and by the time the leg of chicken with dandelion salad arrived – or, as some held, string salad – opinions varied on this point – the hell-brew had so wrought on him that he had begun to lecture Ukridge on his mis-spent life and was urging him in accents audible across the street to go out and get a job and thus acquire sufficient self-respect to enable him to look himself in the face in a mirror without wincing. Not, added Teddy Weeks, with what we all thought uncalled-for offensiveness, that any amount of self-respect was likely to do that. Having said which, he called imperiously for another eight bobs'-worth.

We gazed at one another wanly. However excellent the end towards which all this was tending, there was no denying that it was hard to bear. But policy kept us silent. We recognized that this was Teddy Weeks's evening and that he must be humoured. Victor Beamish said meekly that Teddy had cleared up a lot of points which had been troubling him for a long time. Bertram Fox agreed that there was much in what Teddy had said about the future of the close-up. And even Ukridge, though his haughty soul was seared to its foundations by the latter's personal remarks, promised to take his homily to heart and act upon it at the earliest possible moment.

'You'd better!' said Teddy Weeks, belligerently, biting off the end of one of Barolini's best cigars. 'And there's another thing – don't let me hear of your coming and sneaking people's socks again.'

'Very well, laddie,' said Ukridge, humbly.

'If there is one person in the world that I despise,' said Teddy, bending a red-eyed gaze on the offender, 'it's a snock-seeker – a seek-snocker – a – well, you know what I mean.'

We hastened to assure him that we knew what he meant and he relapsed into a lengthy stupor, from which he emerged three-quarters of an hour later to announce that he didn't know what we intended to do, but that he was going. We said that we were going too, and we paid the bill and did so.

Teddy Weeks's indignation on discovering us gathered about him upon the pavement outside the restaurant was intense, and he expressed it freely. Among other things, he said – which was not true – that he had a reputation to keep up in Soho.

'It's all right, Teddy, old horse,' said Ukridge, soothingly. 'We just thought you would like to have all your old pals round you when you did it.'

'Did it? Did what?'

'Why, had the accident.'

Teddy Weeks glared at him truculently. Then his mood seemed to change abruptly, and he burst into a loud and hearty laugh.

'Well, of all the silly ideas!' he cried, amusedly. 'I'm not going to have an accident. You don't suppose I ever seriously intended to have an accident, do you? It was just my fun.' Then, with another sudden change of mood, he seemed to become a victim to an acute unhappiness. He stroked Ukridge's arm affectionately, and a tear rolled down his cheek. 'Just my fun,' he repeated. 'You don't mind my fun, do you?' he asked, pleadingly. 'You like my fun, don't you? All my fun. Never meant to have an accident at all. Just wanted dinner.' The gay humour of it all overcame his sorrow once more. 'Funniest thing ever heard,' he said cordially. 'Didn't want accident, wanted dinner. Dinner daxident, danner dixident,' he added, driving home his point. 'Well, good night all,' he said, cheerily. And, stepping off the kerb on to a banana-skin, was instantly knocked ten feet by a passing lorry.

'Two ribs and an arm,' said the doctor five minutes later, super-intending the removal proceedings. 'Gently with that stretcher.'

12

BEHAVING BADLY

When it comes to the etiquette of being a good house-guest, the universals are widely agreed – e.g. don't fuss over food, don't pinch anything, don't use all the hot water and try not to loaf about making the place look messy. Furthermore, many will say, don't get drunk – or, at least, don't get very much drunker than your host or hostess.

Wodehouse's comic purpose required that his characters be not especially observant of any such manners, and especially not of that last one.

In The Indiscretions of Archie *(1921) the titular Archie Moffam is wed to Lucille, daughter of millionaire Daniel Brewster who owns New York's finest hotel, the Cosmopolis – and who has a low opinion of his son-in-law on account of some rude remarks made about the hotel to Brewster's face before they became kinfolk. Now a live-in resident with his new bride, Archie gets embroiled in a scene when his old Eton and Oxford friend Lord 'Squiffy' Seacliff – 'always rather a lad for the wassail-bowl' – also checks in to the Cosmopolis. Returning there after dinner and theatre one night, Archie sees Brewster pacing the lobby and recognises trouble.*

There seemed to be something on Mr. Brewster's mind. He came up to Archie with a brooding frown on his square face.

'Who's this man Seacliff?' he demanded, without pre-amble. 'I hear he's a friend of yours.' [...]

'Oh yes. Great pal of mine, Squiffy. We went through Eton, Oxford, and the Bankruptcy Court together. And here's a rummy coincidence. When they examined *me*, I had no assets. And, when they examined Squiffy, *he* had no assets! Rather extraordinary, what?'

Mr. Brewster seemed to be in no mood for discussing coincidences.

'I might have known he was a friend of yours!' he said, bitterly. 'Well, if you want to see him, you'll have to do it outside my hotel.'

'Why, I thought he was stopping here.'

'He is – tonight. To-morrow he can look for some other hotel to break up.'

'Great Scot! Has dear old Squiffy been breaking the place up?'

Mr. Brewster snorted.

'I am informed that this precious friend of yours entered my grill-room at eight o'clock. He must have been completely intoxicated, though the head waiter tells me he noticed nothing at the time.'

Archie nodded approvingly.

'Dear old Squiffy was always like that. It's a gift.

However woozled he might be, it was impossible to detect it with the naked eye. I've seen the dear old chap many a time whiffled to the eyebrows, and looking as sober as a bishop. Soberer! When did it begin to dawn on the lads in the grill-room that the old egg had been pushing the boat out?'

'The head waiter,' said Mr. Brewster, with cold fury, 'tells me that he got a hint of the man's condition when he suddenly got up from his table and went the round of the room, pulling off all the table-cloths, and breaking everything that was on them. He then threw a number of rolls at the diners, and left. He seems to have gone straight to bed.'

'Dashed sensible of him, what? Sound, practical chap, Squiffy. But where on earth did he get the – er – materials?'

'From his room. I made enquiries. He has six large cases in his room.'

'Squiffy always was a chap of infinite resource! . . .'

Bill Oakshott is, as we saw in an earlier extract from Uncle Dynamite, *by no means his Uncle Aylmer's idea of a dream visitor to his country home of Ashenden Manor. And yet, when compared to Pongo Twistleton, in this regard Bill rather comes up trumps – as he relates to Lord Ickenham when they meet again nearer the novel's end.*

'After breakfast this morning, I drove my aunt to Wockley to catch the express to London . . . I was keeping an eye on the road and thinking of this and that, when she suddenly said "Dipsomaniac."'

'Why did she call you a dipsomaniac?'

'She didn't. It turned out she was talking about Pongo . . . Apparently she and Uncle Aylmer found him swigging whisky in the drawing-room.'

'I would not attach too much importance to that. Many of our noblest men swig whisky in drawing-rooms. I do myself.'

'But not all night. Well, you might say all night. What I mean is, I found Pongo in the drawing-room, swigging away, at about one o' clock this morning, and my aunt and uncle appear to have found him there, still swigging, at half-past two. That makes one and a half hours. Give him say half an hour before I came in, and you get two hours of solid swigging. And after my aunt and uncle left he must have started swigging again. Because he was unquestionably stinko after breakfast.'

'I decline to believe that anyone could get stinko at breakfast.'

'I didn't say he did get stinko at breakfast. You're missing the point. My theory is that he swigged all night, got stinko round about six a.m. and continued stinko till the incident occurred.'

'To what incident do you allude?'

'It happened just after breakfast. My aunt was

waiting for me to bring the car round, and Uncle Aylmer made some unpleasant cracks about the hat she was wearing. So she went up to her room to get another, and as she reached the door she heard someone moving about inside. When she went in, there was nobody to be seen, and then suddenly there came a sneeze from the wardrobe, and there was Pongo, crouching on the floor.'

'She was sure?'

'Sure?'

'It wasn't a shoe or a bit of fluff?'

'No, it was Pongo. She says he smiled weakly and said he had looked in to borrow her lipstick. He must have been as tight as an owl. Because, apart from anything else, a glance at Aunt Emily should have told him she hasn't got a lipstick ...'

In 'Jeeves and the Unbidden Guest' (1916) Bertie Wooster is set a task when Lady Malvern, a friend of Aunt Agatha, leaves her son 'Motty' to stay in Bertie's care while she tours the nation's prisons, researching a book. Despite the bother of it, Bertie imagines nonetheless that this will be a simple-enough chore.

About midday Motty's luggage arrived, and soon afterward a large parcel of what I took to be nice books. I brightened up a little when I saw it. It was one of those massive parcels and looked as if it had enough in it to keep the chappie busy for a year. I felt a trifle more cheerful, and I got my Country Gentleman hat and stuck it on my head, and gave the pink tie a twist, and reeled out to take a bite of lunch with one or two of the lads at a neighbouring hostelry; and what with excellent browsing and sluicing and cheery conversation and what-not, the afternoon passed quite happily. By dinner-time I had almost forgotten blighted Motty's existence.

I dined at the club and looked in at a show afterward, and it wasn't till fairly late that I got back to the flat. There were no signs of Motty, and I took it that he had gone to bed.

It seemed rummy to me, though, that the parcel of nice books was still there with the string and paper on it. It looked as if Motty, after seeing mother off at the station, had decided to call it a day.

Jeeves came in with the nightly whisky-and-soda. I could tell by the chappie's manner that he was still upset.

'Lord Pershore gone to bed, Jeeves?' I asked, with reserved hauteur and what-not.

'No, sir. His lordship has not yet returned.'

'Not returned? What do you mean?'

'His lordship came in shortly after six-thirty, and, having dressed, went out again.'

At this moment there was a noise outside the front door, a sort of scrabbling noise, as if somebody were trying to paw his way through the woodwork. Then a sort of thud.

'Better go and see what that is, Jeeves.'

'Very good, sir.'

He went out and came back again.

'If you would not mind stepping this way, sir, I think we might be able to carry him in.'

'Carry him in?'

'His lordship is lying on the mat, sir.'

I went to the front door. The man was right. There was Motty huddled up outside on the floor. He was moaning a bit.

'He's had some sort of dashed fit,' I said. I took another look. 'Jeeves! Someone's been feeding him meat!'

'Sir?'

'He's a vegetarian, you know. He must have been digging into a steak or something. Call up a doctor!'

'I hardly think it will be necessary, sir. If you would take his lordship's legs, while I—'

'Great Scot, Jeeves! You don't think – he can't be—'

'I am inclined to think so, sir.'

And, by Jove, he was right! Once on the right track, you couldn't mistake it. Motty was under the surface.

It was the deuce of a shock.

'You never can tell, Jeeves!'

'Very seldom, sir.'

'Remove the eye of authority and where are you?'

'Precisely, sir.'

'Where is my wandering boy to-night and all that sort of thing, what?'

'It would seem so, sir.'

'Well, we had better bring him in, eh?'

'Yes, sir.'

So we lugged him in, and Jeeves put him to bed, and I lit a cigarette and sat down to think the thing over. I had a kind of foreboding. It seemed to me that I had let myself in for something pretty rocky.

Next morning, after I had sucked down a thoughtful cup of tea, I went into Motty's room to investigate. I expected to find the fellow a wreck, but there he was, sitting up in bed, quite chirpy, reading Gingery stories.

'What ho!' I said.

'What ho!' said Motty.

'What ho! What ho!'

'What ho! What ho! What ho!'

After that it seemed rather difficult to go on with the conversation.

'How are you feeling this morning?' I asked.

'Topping!' replied Motty, blithely and with abandon. 'I say, you know, that fellow of yours – Jeeves, you know – is a corker. I had a most frightful headache when I woke up, and he brought me a sort of rummy dark drink, and it put me right again at once. Said it was his own invention. I must see more of that lad. He seems to me distinctly one of the ones!'

I couldn't believe that this was the same blighter who had sat and sucked his stick the day before.

'You ate something that disagreed with you last night, didn't you?' I said, by way of giving him a chance to slide out of it if he wanted to. But he wouldn't have it, at any price.

'No!' he replied firmly. 'I didn't do anything of the kind. I drank too much! Much too much. Lots and lots too much! And, what's more, I'm going to do it again! I'm going to do it every night. If ever you see me sober, old top,' he said, with a kind of holy exaltation, 'tap me on the shoulder and say, "Tut! Tut!" and I'll apologize and remedy the defect.'

'But I say, you know, what about me?'

'What about you?'

'Well, I'm so to speak, as it were, kind of responsible for you. What I mean to say is, if you go doing this sort of thing I'm apt to get in the soup somewhat.'

'I can't help your troubles,' said Motty firmly. 'Listen to me, old thing: this is the first time in my life that I've had a real chance to yield to the temptations of a great city. What's the use of a great city having temptations if fellows don't yield to them? Makes it so bally discouraging for a great city. Besides, mother told me to keep my eyes open and collect impressions.'

I sat on the edge of the bed. I felt dizzy.

'I know just how you feel, old dear,' said Motty consolingly. 'And, if my principles would permit it, I would simmer down for your sake. But duty first! This is the first time I've been let out alone, and I mean to make the most of it. We're only young once. Why interfere with life's morning? Young man, rejoice in thy youth! Tra-la! What ho!'

Put like that, it did seem reasonable.

13

MORNINGS AFTER

We've all done it. Since happiness can't be pursued in moderation, excess often follows, leading to a predictable sore head once the sun comes up. Wodehouse, thank heavens, offers brilliantly restorative light relief on this subject – and from the outset of his writing career right down to the very end.

Here, in Piccadilly Jim *(1919), man-about-town Jimmy Crocker tries to explain what went wrong the night before to the family butler, Bayliss.*

Jimmy Crocker was a tall and well-knit young man who later on in the day would no doubt be at least passably good-looking. At the moment an unbecoming pallor marred his face, and beneath his eyes were marks that suggested that he had slept little and ill. He stood at the foot of the stairs, yawning cavernously.

'Bayliss,' he said, 'have you been painting yourself yellow?'

'No, sir.'

'Strange! Your face looks a bright gamboge to me, and your outlines wobble. Bayliss, never mix your drinks. I say this to you as a friend. Is there anyone in the morning-room?'

'No, Mr. James.'

'Speak softly, Bayliss, for I am not well. I am conscious of a strange weakness. Lead me to the morning-room, then, and lay me gently on a sofa. These are the times that try men's souls.'

The sun was now shining strongly through the windows of the morning-room. Bayliss lowered the shades. Jimmy Crocker sank onto the sofa, and closed his eyes.

'Bayliss.'

'Sir?'

'A conviction is stealing over me that I am about to expire.'

'Shall I bring you a little breakfast, Mr. James?'

A strong shudder shook Jimmy.

'Don't be flippant, Bayliss,' he protested. 'Try to cure yourself of this passion for being funny at the wrong time. Your comedy is good, but tact is a finer quality than humour. Perhaps you think I have forgotten that morning when I was feeling just as I do today and you came to my bedside and asked me if I would like a nice rasher of ham. I haven't and I never shall. You may bring me a brandy-and-soda. Not a large one. A couple of bath-tubs full will be enough.'

'Very good, Mr. James.'

'And now leave me, Bayliss, for I would be alone. I

have to make a series of difficult and exhaustive tests to ascertain whether I am still alive.'

The properly penitent over-indulger must first be honest about what did the damage. This is from 'Up from the Depths' in Nothing Serious *(1950). Our hero Ambrose Gussett drops by of a morning on tennis professional and romantic rival Dwight Messmore, finding him off-colour and regrettably full of half-baked excuses.*

It was plain to Ambrose's experienced eye that the man was not in his customary vigorous health. He was wearing about his forehead a towel which appeared to have ice in it, and his complexion was a curious greenish yellow.

'Come in,' said Dwight Messmore, speaking in a hollow, husky voice, like a spirit at a *séance*. 'I was just going to send for you. Walk on tip-toe, do you mind, and speak very softly. I am on the point of expiring.'

He lowered himself into a chair, and Ambrose gently placed a thermometer in his mouth.

'Can we think of anything that can have caused this little indisposition?' he asked.

'Charcoal poisoning,' said Dwight Messmore promptly. 'I gave a little party last night to a few fellows to celebrate my making the Davis Cup team—'

'Did we drink anything?'

'Not a thing. Well, just a bottle or two of champagne, and liqueurs . . . brandy, chartreuse, benedictine, curaçao,

97

créme de menthe, kummel and so forth . ... and of course whisky. But nothing more. It was practically a teetotal evening. No, what did the trick was that charcoal. As you are probably aware, the stuff they sell you as caviare in this country isn't caviare. It's whitefish roe, and they colour it with powdered charcoal. Well, you can't sit up half the night eating powdered charcoal without paying the penalty.'

The comedy of 'The Luck of the Stiffhams' from Young Men in Spats *hinges on the efforts of Adolphus 'Stiffy' Stiffham to sneak into the home of Lord Wivelscombe – whose daughter Stiffy adores – and retrieve an abusive letter (written in pique and mailed over-hastily by Stiffy) before his Lordship has a chance to read and digest the disastrous contents. Stiffy manages to make it into Wivelscombe's bedroom and underneath a table, unseen – at which point his luck really kicks in, for it turns out the Lord is feeling less than usually attentive this particular morning.*

As far as Stiffy could gather from the look of the legs moving about in his vicinity, it was the butler who had returned, presumably with coffee and foodstuffs. He could just see the lower section of a pair of striped trousers, as worn by butlers.

Then the door opened once more, this time to admit a pair of pyjamaed legs terminating in bedroom slippers, and reason told him that this must be old Wivelscombe. When the pyjamas passed from his view to appear again under the table within a couple of inches of his nose, their owner having sunk heavily into a chair, he knew that he had been right, and he is not ashamed to confess that he was conscious of a certain qualm. Seeing at such close range the foot which had once landed so forcefully on his trouser seat was, he tells me, an unnerving experience.

A bit of dialogue now unshipped itself in the upper regions. The butler started it.

'Good morning, m'lord. Shall I assist your lordship to a little eggs and bacon?'

The table shook as the aged peer shuddered strongly.

'Don't try to be funny, Gascoigne. There is a time to speak of eggs and a time not to speak of eggs. At the moment, I would prefer to try to forget that there are such things in the world. What you can bring me – and dashed quick, too – is a very hot, very strong cup of coffee, liberally laced with old brandy, and a very dry slice of toast.'

The butler coughed in rather an unpleasant and censorious manner.

'Did your lordship exceed last night?'

'Certainly not.'

'Did your lordship imbibe champagne?'

'The merest spot.'

'A bottle?'

'It may have been a bottle.'

'Two bottles?'

'Yes. Possibly two bottles.'

The butler coughed again.

'I shall inform Doctor Spelvin.'

'Don't be a cad, Gascoigne.'

'He has expressly forbidden your lordship champagne.'

'Tchah!'

'I need scarcely remind your lordship that champagne brings your lordship out in spots.'

Old Wivelscombe barked querulously.

'I wish to goodness you wouldn't stand there babbling about champagne. It is a word that I do not wish to have mentioned in my presence.'

'Very good, m'lord,' said the butler stiffly. 'Your coffee, m'lord. The dry toast is at your lordship's elbow.'

There was a pause. From the sloshing sound which broke out above him at this point, Stiffy deduced that old Wivelscombe was drinking the coffee. The theory was borne out by the fact that when he spoke again it was in a stronger voice.

'It's no good your looking like that, Gascoigne. After all, what's an occasional binge? It's a poor heart that never rejoices.'

'At your lordship's age, all binges are highly injudicious.'

'What do you mean, my age? A man is as old as he feels.'

'Very good, m'lord.'

'Where you go wrong, Gascoigne – where you make your bloomer is in assuming that I have a hangover this morning. Nothing could be further from the truth. I feel like a two-year-old. Look at my hand. Steady as a rock.'

Apparently, at this point, old Wivelscombe ventured on a physical demonstration. A napkin came fluttering down on the floor.

'Very wobbly, m'lord.'

'Nothing of the kind,' said old Wivelscombe testily. 'I dropped that napkin on purpose, just to show you how easily I could pick it up. See, Gascoigne. I will now pick up the napkin.'

But he didn't. He stooped down and his fingers touched the thing, but as they did so he suddenly found himself looking into Stiffy's bulging eyes. There was an embarrassing pause for a moment: then his face shot up out of sight and Stiffy heard him gulp.

'Gascoigne!'

'M'lord?'

'Gascoigne, there's a ghost under the table.'

'Very good, m'lord.'

Crocker, Messmore, Wivelscombe – Wodehouse shows them all floundering in the sullied wake of what they have done to themselves. If only they had resort to a cure! If only they could call on the expertise of Jeeves . . . The happy beneficiary of that share of fortune, however, is Bertie Wooster – though he is generous with his luck, as here, in The Mating Season *(1949), when he takes pity on a stricken visitor: poor old Claude Cattermole ('Catsmeat') Pirbright.*

[Catsmeat] sank into a chair and closed his eyes, and for some moments remained motionless. Then, as if a bomb had suddenly exploded inside the bean, he shot up with a stifled cry, clasping his temples, and I began to see daylight. His deportment, so plainly that of a man aware that only prompt action in the nick of time has prevented his head splitting in half, told me that we had been mistaken in supposing that this living corpse had got that way purely through disappointed love. I touched the bell, and Jeeves appeared.

'One of your special mornings-after, if you please, Jeeves.'

'Very good, sir.'

He shimmered out, and I subjected Catsmeat to a keen glance. I am told by those who know that there are six varieties of hangover – the Broken Compass, the Sewing Machine, the Comet, the Atomic, the Cement Mixer, and the Gremlin Boogie, and his manner suggested that he had got them all.

'So you were lathered last night?' I said.

'I was perhaps a mite polluted,' he admitted.

'Jeeves has gone for one of his revivers.'

'Thank you, Bertie, thank you,' said Catsmeat in a low, soft voice, and closed his eyes again.

Catsmeat is greatly revived by the contents of the glass that Jeeves fetches him; and Bertie is not a bit surprised. As he remarks elsewhere (in The Inimitable Jeeves*), 'There's no doubt that Jeeves's pick-me-ups will produce immediate results in anything short of an Egyptian mummy.'*

In the 1916 short story 'Jeeves Takes Charge' *Bertie spills the beans on his first experience of a 'dynamite special', and also on the mystery of its contents, revealed to him on the very day that Jeeves entered his service.*

'I shall always remember the morning he came. It so happened that the night before I had been present at a rather cheery little supper, and I was feeling pretty rocky. On top of this I was trying to read a book Florence Craye had given me ... She was a girl with a wonderful profile, but steeped to the gills in serious purpose. I can't give you a better idea of the way things stood than by telling you that the book she'd given me to read was called 'Types of Ethical Theory,' and that when I opened it at random I struck a page beginning:

"The postulate or common understanding involved in speech is certainly co-extensive, in the obligation it carries, with the social organism of which language is the instrument, and the ends of which it is an effort to subserve."

All perfectly true, no doubt; but not the sort of thing to spring on a lad with a morning head.

I was doing my best to skim through this bright little volume when the bell rang. I crawled off the sofa and opened the door. A kind of darkish sort of respectful Johnnie stood without.

'I was sent by the agency, sir,' he said. 'I was given to understand that you required a valet.'

I'd have preferred an undertaker; but I told him to stagger in, and he floated noiselessly through the doorway like a healing zephyr. That impressed me from the start. Meadowes had had flat feet and used to clump. This fellow didn't seem to have any feet at all. He just streamed in. He had a grave, sympathetic face, as if he, too, knew what it was to sup with the lads.

'Excuse me, sir,' he said gently.

Then he seemed to flicker, and wasn't there any longer. I heard him moving about in the kitchen, and presently he came back with a glass on a tray.

'If you would drink this, sir,' he said, with a kind of bedside manner, rather like the royal doctor shooting the bracer into the sick prince. 'It is a little preparation of my own invention. It is the Worcester Sauce that gives it its colour. The raw egg makes it nutritious. The red pepper gives it its bite. Gentlemen have told me they have found it extremely invigorating after a late evening.'

I would have clutched at anything that looked like a life-line that morning. I swallowed the stuff. For a moment I felt as if somebody had touched off a bomb inside the old bean and was strolling down my throat with a lighted torch, and then everything seemed suddenly to get all right. The sun shone in through the window; birds twittered in the tree-tops; and, generally speaking, hope dawned once more.

'You're engaged!' I said, as soon as I could say anything.

I perceived clearly that this cove was one of the world's wonders, the sort no home should be without.

'Thank you, sir. My name is Jeeves.'

'You can start in at once?'

'Immediately, sir . . .'

And with that, the legend takes wing. As many have observed, Jeeves's recipe is not so dissimilar from the 'Prairie Oyster' remedy later popularised by Christopher Isherwood's literary creation of the 1930s, Sally Bowles. And, while the magic effects described by Bertie make for a lovely and inspiring thought, for most of us a couple of ibuprofen taken tactically make for a prettier sight and, probably, a better outcome.

Still, the thought is hard to resist when Wodehouse, through the medium of Bertie, evokes those effects as he does in Right Ho Jeeves:

For perhaps the split part of a second nothing happens. It is as though all Nature waited breathless. Then, suddenly, it is as if the Last Trump had sounded and Judgment Day set in with unusual severity.

Bonfires burst out in all parts of the frame. The abdomen becomes heavily charged with molten lava. A great wind seems to blow through the world, and the subject is aware of something resembling a steam hammer striking the back of the head. During this phase, the ears ring loudly, the eyeballs rotate and there is a tingling about the brow.

And then, just as you are feeling that you ought to ring up your lawyer and see that your affairs are in order before it is too late, the whole situation seems to clarify. The wind drops. The ears cease to ring. Birds twitter. Brass bands start playing. The sun comes up over the horizon with a jerk.

And a moment later all you are conscious of is a great peace.

As I drained the glass now, new life seemed to burgeon within me. I remember Jeeves, who, however much he may go off the rails at times in the matter of dress clothes and in his advice to those in love, has always had a neat turn of phrase, once speaking of someone rising on stepping-stones of his dead self to higher things. It was that way with me now. I felt that the Bertram Wooster who lay propped up against the pillows had become a better, stronger, finer Bertram.

'Thank you, Jeeves,' I said.

'Not at all, sir.'

'That touched the exact spot. I am now able to cope with life's problems.'

'I am gratified to hear it, sir.'

14

JEEVES PARTAKES!

In Wodehouse's 1919 collection My Man Jeeves *is the American-set story 'The Aunt and the Sluggard', memorable for its account of Jeeves – who usually perches on a high slope far above the fray of Bertie's binges – revealing himself to be a bit of a dark horse.*

It begins with Rocky Todd, a languid Long Island poet, coming to his old friend Bertie with a poser: his Aunt Isabel Rockmetteller from Illinois (who considers herself an invalid but dreams of Manhattan's 'wonderful gay life'), who is prepared to gift Rocky a hefty monthly allowance, but only on the condition that he will move from Long Island to Manhattan, there to plunge into the city's social hubbub, and write to her weekly letters describing all the fabulous parties and sprees – descriptions through which Aunt Isabel expects to live vicariously. Though Bertie regards this as a 'pretty soft' offer, Rocky is downcast, for he 'loathes' the liveliness of New York City to the bottom of his poetic soul ('The very thought of staying more than a day in it makes me sick'). Evidently, then, a third intelligence must be applied to the problem.

'What do you suggest, Jeeves?' I said.
Jeeves cleared his throat respectfully.

'The crux of the matter would appear to be, sir, that Mr. Todd is obliged by the conditions under which the money is delivered into his possession to write Miss Rockmetteller long and detailed letters relating to his movements, and the only method by which this can be accomplished, if Mr. Todd adheres to his expressed intention of remaining in the country, is for Mr. Todd to induce some second party to gather the actual experiences which Miss Rockmetteller wishes reported to her, and to convey these to him in the shape of a careful report, on which it would be possible for him, with the aid of his imagination, to base the suggested correspondence.'

Having got which off the old diaphragm, Jeeves was silent. Rocky looked at me in a helpless sort of way. He hasn't been brought up on Jeeves as I have, and he isn't on to his curves.

'Could he put it a little clearer, Bertie?' he said. 'I thought at the start it was going to make sense, but it kind of flickered. What's the idea?'

'My dear old man, perfectly simple. I knew we could stand on Jeeves. All you've got to do is to get somebody to go round the town for you and take a few notes, and then you work the notes up into letters. That's it, isn't it, Jeeves?'

'Precisely, sir.'

The light of hope gleamed in Rocky's eyes. He looked at Jeeves in a startled way, dazed by the man's vast intellect.

'But who would do it?' he said. 'It would have to be a pretty smart sort of man, a man who would notice things.'

'Jeeves!' I said. 'Let Jeeves do it.'

'But would he?'

'You would do it, wouldn't you, Jeeves?'

For the first time in our long connection I observed Jeeves almost smile. The corner of his mouth curved quite a quarter of an inch, and for a moment his eye ceased to look like a meditative fish's.

'I should be delighted to oblige, sir. As a matter of fact, I have already visited some of New York's places of interest on my evening out, and it would be most enjoyable to make a practice of the pursuit.'

'Fine! I know exactly what your aunt wants to hear about, Rocky. She wants an earful of cabaret stuff. The place you ought to go to first, Jeeves, is Reigelheimer's. It's on Forty-second Street. Anybody will show you the way.'

Jeeves shook his head.

'Pardon me, sir. People are no longer going to Reigelheimer's. The place at the moment is Frolics on the Roof.'

'You see?' I said to Rocky. 'Leave it to Jeeves. He knows.'

It isn't often that you find an entire group of your fellow humans happy in this world; but our little circle was certainly an example of the fact that it can be done.

We were all full of beans. Everything went absolutely right from the start.

Jeeves was happy, partly because he loves to exercise his giant brain, and partly because he was having a corking time among the bright lights. I saw him one night at the Midnight Revels. He was sitting at a table on the edge of the dancing floor, doing himself remarkably well with a fat cigar and a bottle of the best. I'd never imagined he could look so nearly human . . .

15

'WHAT A BEAUTIFUL WORLD THIS IS, BERTIE'

Arguably the greatest and most peerlessly sustained passage of comic genius in all of Wodehouse is the following – from Right Ho, Jeeves *(1934), in which Bertie Wooster presses his old school friend Gussie Fink-Nottle into the service of Aunt Dahlia, despatching Gussie to stay at Dahlia's country seat of Brinkley Court and, worse, to perform the grim chore of handing out the annual prizes to pupils of Market Snodsbury Grammar School.*

Still, there is an incentive for Gussie, in that also staying at Brinkley Court is a whimsical, 'saucer-eyed' girl named Madeline Bassett with whom he has fallen in love at first sight. But Gussie, a solitary newt-fancier, naturally nervy and timid, is utterly useless at pitching woo to Madeline; and so Bertie kindly decides to take Gussie's case in hand, quite certain he is better equipped for the job than Jeeves.

After establishing, with some difficulty, that Madeline is in fact fairly keen on Gussie, still Bertie cannot rouse his friend to 'take another whack at her'. Worse, Gussie, painfully unused to public speaking, remains in bits at the prospect of his duties at Market

Snodsbury School. Thus Bertie resolves that Gussie – a teetotaller whose regular tipple is orange juice – must have something stronger to boost his spirits: a shot or two of 'the right stuff' in liquid form. Since Gussie, however, will not take a strong drink of his own volition, then the deed must be done by deception. And since Jeeves refuses to get involved in this particular caper, the spiking duties devolve upon Bertram Wooster.

Now read on . . .

'Leave me, Bertie. Push off. That's all I ask you to do. Push off . . . Ladies and gentlemen,' said Gussie, in a low, soliloquizing sort of way, 'I do not propose to detain this auspicious occasion long—'

It was a thoughtful Wooster who walked away and left him at it. More than ever I was congratulating myself on having had the sterling good sense to make all my arrangements so that I could press a button and set things moving at an instant's notice.

Until now, you see, I had rather entertained a sort of hope that when I had revealed to him the Bassett's mental attitude, Nature would have done the rest, bracing him up to such an extent that artificial stimulants would not be required. Because, naturally, a chap doesn't want to have to sprint about country houses lugging jugs of orange juice, unless it is absolutely essential.

But now I saw that I must carry on as planned. The total absence of pep, ginger, and the right spirit which the man had displayed during these conversational exchanges convinced me that the strongest measures would be necessary. Immediately upon leaving him, therefore, I proceeded to the pantry, waited till the butler had removed himself elsewhere, and nipped in and secured the vital jug. A few moments later, after a wary passage of the stairs, I was in my room. And the first thing I saw there was Jeeves, fooling about with trousers.

He gave the jug a look which – wrongly, as it was to turn out – I diagnosed as censorious. I drew myself up a bit. I intended to have no rot from the fellow.

'Yes, Jeeves?'

'Sir?'

'You have the air of one about to make a remark, Jeeves.'

'Oh, no, sir. I note that you are in possession of Mr. Fink-Nottle's orange juice. I was merely about to observe that in my opinion it would be injudicious to add spirit to it.'

'That is a remark, Jeeves, and it is precisely—'

'Because I have already attended to the matter, sir.'

'What?'

'Yes, sir. I decided, after all, to acquiesce in your wishes.'

I stared at the man, astounded. I was deeply moved. Well, I mean, wouldn't any chap who had been going about thinking that the old feudal spirit was dead and then suddenly found it wasn't have been deeply moved?

'Jeeves,' I said, 'I am touched.'

'Thank you, sir.'

'Touched and gratified.'

'Thank you very much, sir.'

'But what caused this change of heart?'

'I chanced to encounter Mr. Fink-Nottle in the garden, sir, while you were still in bed, and we had a brief conversation.'

'And you came away feeling that he needed a bracer?'

'Very much so, sir. His attitude struck me as defeatist.'

I nodded.

'I felt the same. "Defeatist" sums it up to a nicety. Did you tell him his attitude struck you as defeatist?'

'Yes, sir.'

'But it didn't do any good?'

'No, sir.'

'Very well, then, Jeeves. We must act. How much gin did you put in the jug?'

'A liberal tumblerful, sir.'

'Would that be a normal dose for an adult defeatist, do you think?'

'I fancy it should prove adequate, sir.'

'I wonder. We must not spoil the ship for a ha'porth of tar. I think I'll add just another fluid ounce or so.'

'I would not advocate it, sir. In the case of Lord Brancaster's parrot—'

'You are falling into your old error, Jeeves, of thinking that Gussie is a parrot. Fight against this. I shall add the oz.'

'Very good, sir.'

'And, by the way, Jeeves, Mr. Fink-Nottle is in the market for bright, clean stories to use in his speech. Do you know any?'

'I know a story about two Irishmen, sir.'

'Pat and Mike?'

'Yes, sir.'

'Who were walking along Broadway?'

'Yes, sir.'

'Just what he wants. Any more?'

'No, sir.'

'Well, every little helps. You had better go and tell it to him.'

'Very good, sir.'

He passed from the room, and I unscrewed the flask and tilted into the jug a generous modicum of its contents. And scarcely had I done so, when there came to my ears the sound of footsteps without. I had only just time to shove the jug behind the photograph of Uncle Tom on the mantelpiece before the door opened and in came Gussie, curveting like a circus horse.

'What-ho, Bertie,' he said. 'What-ho, what-ho, what-ho, and again what-ho. What a beautiful world this is, Bertie. One of the nicest I ever met.'

I stared at him, speechless. We Woosters are as quick

as lightning, and I saw at once that something had happened.

I mean to say, I told you about him walking round in circles. I recorded what passed between us on the lawn. And if I portrayed the scene with anything like adequate skill, the picture you will have retained of this Fink-Nottle will have been that of a nervous wreck, sagging at the knees, green about the gills, and picking feverishly at the lapels of his coat in an ecstasy of craven fear. In a word, defeatist. Gussie, during that interview, had, in fine, exhibited all the earmarks of one licked to a custard.

Vastly different was the Gussie who stood before me now. Self-confidence seemed to ooze from the fellow's every pore. His face was flushed, there was a jovial light in his eyes, the lips were parted in a swashbuckling smile. And when with a genial hand he sloshed me on the back before I could sidestep, it was as if I had been kicked by a mule.

'Well, Bertie,' he proceeded, as blithely as a linnet without a thing on his mind, 'you will be glad to hear that you were right. Your theory has been tested and proved correct. I feel like a fighting cock.'

My brain ceased to reel. I saw all.

'Have you been having a drink?'

'I have. As you advised. Unpleasant stuff. Like medicine. Burns your throat, too, and makes one as thirsty as the dickens. How anyone can mop it up, as you do, for pleasure, beats me. Still, I would be the last to deny that it tunes up the system. I could bite a tiger.'

'What did you have?'

'Whisky. At least, that was the label on the decanter, and I have no reason to suppose that a woman like your aunt – staunch, true-blue, British – would deliberately deceive the public. If she labels her decanters Whisky, then I consider that we know where we are.'

'A whisky and soda, eh? You couldn't have done better.'

'Soda?' said Gussie thoughtfully. 'I knew there was something I had forgotten.'

'Didn't you put any soda in it?'

'It never occurred to me. I just nipped into the dining-room and drank out of the decanter.'

'How much?'

'Oh, about ten swallows. Twelve, maybe. Or fourteen. Say sixteen medium-sized gulps. Gosh, I'm thirsty.'

He moved over to the wash-stand and drank deeply out of the water bottle. I cast a covert glance at Uncle Tom's photograph behind his back. For the first time since it had come into my life, I was glad that it was so large. It hid its secret well. If Gussie had caught sight of that jug of orange juice, he would unquestionably have been on to it like a knife.

'Well, I'm glad you're feeling braced,' I said.

He moved buoyantly from the wash-hand stand, and endeavoured to slosh me on the back again. Foiled by my nimble footwork, he staggered to the bed and sat down upon it.

'Braced? Did I say I could bite a tiger?'

'You did.'

'Make it two tigers. I could chew holes in a steel door. What an ass you must have thought me out there in the garden. I see now you were laughing in your sleeve.'

'No, no.'

'Yes,' insisted Gussie. 'That very sleeve,' he said, pointing. 'And I don't blame you. I can't imagine why I made all that fuss about a potty job like distributing prizes at a rotten little country grammar school. Can you imagine, Bertie? Exactly. Nor can I imagine. There's simply nothing to it. I just shin up on the platform, drop a few gracious words, hand the little blighters their prizes, and hop down again, admired by all. Not a suggestion of split trousers from start to finish. I mean, why should anybody split his trousers? I can't imagine. Can you imagine?'

'No.'

'Nor can I imagine. I shall be a riot. I know just the sort of stuff that's needed – simple, manly, optimistic stuff straight from the shoulder. This shoulder,' said Gussie, tapping. 'Why I was so nervous this morning I can't imagine. For anything simpler than distributing a few footling books to a bunch of grimy-faced kids I can't imagine. Still, for some reason I can't imagine, I was feeling a little nervous, but now I feel fine, Bertie – fine,

fine, fine – and I say this to you as an old friend. Because that's what you are, old man, when all the smoke has cleared away – an old friend. I don't think I've ever met an older friend. How long have you been an old friend of mine, Bertie?'

'Oh, years and years.'

'Imagine! Though, of course, there must have been a time when you were a new friend ... Hullo, the luncheon gong. Come on, old friend.'

And, rising from the bed like a performing flea, he made for the door.

I followed rather pensively. What had occurred was, of course, so much velvet, as you might say. I mean, I had wanted a braced Fink-Nottle – indeed, all my plans had had a braced Fink-Nottle as their end and aim – but I found myself wondering a little whether the Fink-Nottle now sliding down the banister wasn't, perhaps, a shade too braced. His demeanour seemed to me that of a man who might quite easily throw bread about at lunch.

Fortunately, however, the settled gloom of those round him exercised a restraining effect upon him at the table. It would have needed a far more plastered man to have been rollicking at such a gathering. I had told the Bassett that there were aching hearts in Brinkley Court, and it now looked probable that there would shortly be aching tummies. Anatole, I learned, had retired to his bed with a fit of the vapours, and the meal now before us had been cooked by the kitchen maid – as C_3 a performer as ever wielded a skillet.

This, coming on top of their other troubles, induced in the company a pretty unanimous silence – a solemn stillness, as you might say – which even Gussie did not seem prepared to break. Except, therefore, for one short snatch of song on his part, nothing untoward marked the occasion, and presently we rose, with instructions from Aunt Dahlia to put on festal raiment and be at Market Snodsbury not later than 3.30. This leaving me ample time to smoke a gasper or two in a shady bower beside the lake, I did so, repairing to my room round about the hour of three.

Jeeves was on the job, adding the final polish to the old topper, and I was about to apprise him of the latest developments in the matter of Gussie, when he forestalled me by observing that the latter had only just concluded an agreeable visit to the Wooster bedchamber.

'I found Mr. Fink-Nottle seated here when I arrived to lay out your clothes, sir.'

'Indeed, Jeeves? Gussie was in here, was he?'

'Yes, sir. He left only a few moments ago. He is driving to the school with Mr. and Mrs. Travers in the large car.'

'Did you give him your story of the two Irishmen?'

'Yes, sir. He laughed heartily.'

'Good. Had you any other contributions for him?'

'I ventured to suggest that he might mention to the young gentlemen that education is a drawing out, not a putting in. The late Lord Brancaster was much addicted to presenting prizes at schools, and he invariably employed this dictum.'

'And how did he react to that?'

'He laughed heartily, sir.'

'This surprised you, no doubt? This practically incessant merriment, I mean.'

'Yes, sir.'

'You thought it odd in one who, when you last saw him, was well up in Group A of the defeatists.'

'Yes, sir.'

'There is a ready explanation, Jeeves. Since you last saw him, Gussie has been on a bender. He's as tight as an owl.'

'Indeed, sir?'

'Absolutely. His nerve cracked under the strain, and he sneaked into the dining-room and started mopping the stuff up like a vacuum cleaner. Whisky would seem to be what he filled the radiator with. I gather that he used up most of the decanter. Golly, Jeeves, it's lucky he didn't get at that laced orange juice on top of that, what?'

'Extremely, sir.'

I eyed the jug. Uncle Tom's photograph had fallen into the fender, and it was standing there right out in the open, where Gussie couldn't have helped seeing it. Mercifully, it was empty now.

'It was a most prudent act on your part, if I may say so, sir, to dispose of the orange juice.'

I stared at the man.

'What? Didn't you?'

'No, sir.'

'Jeeves, let us get this clear. Was it not you who threw away that OJ?'

'No, sir. I assumed, when I entered the room and found the pitcher empty, that you had done so.'

We looked at each other, awed. Two minds with but a single thought.

'I very much fear, sir—'

'So do I, Jeeves.'

'It would seem almost certain—'

'Quite certain. Weigh the facts. Sift the evidence. The jug was standing on the mantelpiece, for all eyes to behold. Gussie had been complaining of thirst. You found him in here, laughing heartily. I think that there can be little doubt, Jeeves, that the entire contents of that jug are at this moment reposing on top of the existing cargo in that already brilliantly lit man's interior. Disturbing, Jeeves.'

'Most disturbing, sir.'

'Let us face the position, forcing ourselves to be calm. You inserted in that jug – shall we say a tumblerful of the right stuff?'

'Fully a tumblerful, sir.'

'And I added of my plenty about the same amount.'

'Yes, sir.'

'And in two shakes of a duck's tail Gussie, with all that lapping about inside him, will be distributing the prizes at Market Snodsbury Grammar School before an audience of all that is fairest and most refined in the county.'

'Yes, sir.'

'It seems to me, Jeeves, that the ceremony may be one fraught with considerable interest.'

'Yes, sir.'

'What, in your opinion, will the harvest be?'

'One finds it difficult to hazard a conjecture, sir.'

'You mean imagination boggles?'

'Yes, sir.'

I inspected my imagination. He was right. It boggled.

'And yet, Jeeves,' I said, twiddling a thoughtful steering wheel, 'there is always the bright side.'

Some twenty minutes had elapsed, and having picked the honest fellow up outside the front door, I was driving in the two-seater to the picturesque town of Market Snodsbury. Since we had parted – he to go to his lair and fetch his hat, I to remain in my room and complete the formal costume – I had been doing some close thinking.

The results of this I now proceeded to hand on to him.

'However dark the prospect may be, Jeeves, however murkily the storm clouds may seem to gather, a keen eye can usually discern the blue bird. It is bad, no doubt, that Gussie should be going, some ten minutes from now, to distribute prizes in a state of advanced intoxication, but we must never forget that these things cut both ways.'

'You imply, sir—'

'Precisely. I am thinking of him in his capacity of wooer. All this ought to have put him in rare shape for offering his hand in marriage. I shall be vastly surprised if it won't turn him into a sort of caveman. Have you ever seen James Cagney in the movies?'

'Yes, sir.'

'Something on those lines.'

I heard him cough, and sniped him with a sideways glance. He was wearing that informative look of his.

'Then you have not heard, sir?'

'Eh?'

'You are not aware that a marriage has been arranged and will shortly take place between Mr. Fink-Nottle and Miss Bassett?'

'What?'

'Yes, sir.'

'When did this happen?'

'Shortly after Mr. Fink-Nottle had left your room, sir.'

'Ah! In the post-orange-juice era?'

'Yes, sir.'

'But are you sure of your facts? How do you know?'

'My informant was Mr. Fink-Nottle himself, sir. He appeared anxious to confide in me. His story was some-what incoherent, but I had no difficulty in apprehending its substance. Prefacing his remarks with the statement that this was a beautiful world, he laughed heartily and said that he had become formally engaged.'

'No details?'

'No, sir.'

'But one can picture the scene.'

'Yes, sir.'

'I mean, imagination doesn't boggle.'

'No, sir.'

And it didn't. I could see exactly what must have happened. Insert a liberal dose of mixed spirits in a normally abstemious man, and he becomes a force. He does not stand around, twiddling his fingers and stammering. He acts. I had no doubt that Gussie must have reached for the Bassett and clasped her to him like a stevedore handling a sack of coals.

And one could readily envisage the effect of that sort of thing on a girl of romantic mind.

'Well, well, well, Jeeves.'

'Yes, sir.'

'This is splendid news.'

'Yes, sir.'

'You see now how right I was.'

'Yes, sir.'

'It must have been rather an eye-opener for you, watching me handle this case.'

'Yes, sir.'

'The simple, direct method never fails.'

'No, sir.'

'Whereas the elaborate does.'

'Yes, sir.'

'Right ho, Jeeves.'

We had arrived at the main entrance of Market Snodsbury Grammar School. I parked the car, and went in, well content . . .

The Grammar School at Market Snodsbury had, I understood, been built somewhere in the year 1416, and, as with so many of these ancient foundations, there still seemed to brood over its Great Hall, where the afternoon's festivities were to take place, not a little of the fug of the centuries. It was the hottest day of the summer, and though somebody had opened a tentative window or two, the atmosphere remained distinctive and individual.

In this hall the youth of Market Snodsbury had been eating its daily lunch for a matter of five hundred years, and the flavour lingered. The air was sort of heavy and languorous, if you know what I mean, with the scent of Young England and boiled beef and carrots.

Aunt Dahlia, who was sitting with a bevy of the local nibs in the second row, sighted me as I entered and waved to me to join her, but I was too smart for that. I wedged myself in among the standees at the back, leaning up against a chap who, from the aroma, might have been a corn chandler or something on that order. The essence of strategy on these occasions is to be as near the door as possible.

The hall was gaily decorated with flags and coloured paper, and the eye was further refreshed by the spectacle of a mixed drove of boys, parents, and what not, the former running a good deal to shiny faces and Eton collars, the latter stressing the black-satin note rather when female, and looking as if their coats were too tight, if male. And presently there was some applause – sporadic, Jeeves has since told me it was – and I saw Gussie being steered by a bearded bloke in a gown to a seat in the middle of the platform.

And I confess that as I beheld him and felt that there but for the grace of God went Bertram Wooster, a shudder ran through the frame. It all reminded me so vividly of the time I had addressed that girls' school.

Of course, looking at it dispassionately, you may say that for horror and peril there is no comparison between an almost human audience like the one before me and a mob of small girls with pigtails down their backs, and this, I concede, is true. Nevertheless, the spectacle was enough to make me feel like a fellow watching a pal going over Niagara Falls in a barrel, and the thought of what I had escaped caused everything for a moment to go black and swim before my eyes.

When I was able to see clearly once more, I perceived that Gussie was now seated. He had his hands on his knees, with his elbows out at right angles, like a nigger minstrel of the old school about to ask Mr. Bones why a chicken crosses the road, and he was staring before him with a smile so fixed and pebble-beached that I should have thought that anybody could have guessed that there sat one in whom the old familiar juice was splashing up against the back of the front teeth.

In fact, I saw Aunt Dahlia, who, having assisted at so many hunting dinners in her time, is second to none as a judge of the symptoms, give a start and gaze long and earnestly. And she was just saying something to Uncle Tom on her left when the bearded bloke stepped to the footlights and started making a speech. From the fact that he spoke as if he had a hot potato in his mouth without getting the raspberry from the lads in the ringside seats, I deduced that he must be the head master.

With his arrival in the spotlight, a sort of perspiring resignation seemed to settle on the audience. Personally, I snuggled up against the chandler and let my attention wander. The speech was on the subject of the doings of the school during the past term, and this part of a prize-giving is always apt rather to fail to grip the visiting stranger.

I mean, you know how it is. You're told that J. B. Brewster has won an Exhibition for Classics at Cat's, Cambridge, and you feel that it's one of those stories where you can't see how funny it is unless you really know the fellow. And the same applies to G. Bullett being awarded the Lady Jane Wix Scholarship at the Birmingham College of Veterinary Science.

In fact, I and the corn chandler, who was looking a

bit fagged I thought, as if he had had a hard morning chandling the corn, were beginning to doze lightly when things suddenly brisked up, bringing Gussie into the picture for the first time.

'Today,' said the bearded bloke, 'we are all happy to welcome as the guest of the afternoon, Mr. Fitz-Wattle—'

At the beginning of the address, Gussie had subsided into a sort of daydream, with his mouth hanging open. About half-way through, faint signs of life had begun to show. And for the last few minutes he had been trying to cross one leg over the other and failing and having another shot and failing again. But only now did he exhibit any real animation. He sat up with a jerk.

'Fink-Nottle,' he said, opening his eyes.

'Fitz-Nottle.'

'Fink-Nottle.'

'I should say Fink-Nottle.'

'Of course you should, you silly ass,' said Gussie genially. 'All right, get on with it.'

And closing his eyes, he began trying to cross his legs again.

I could see that this little spot of friction had rattled the bearded bloke a bit. He stood for a moment fumbling at the fungus with a hesitating hand. But they make these head masters of tough stuff. The weakness passed. He came back nicely and carried on.

'We are all happy, I say, to welcome as the guest of the afternoon, Mr. Fink-Nottle, who has kindly consented to award the prizes. This task, as you know, is one that should have devolved upon that well-beloved and vigorous member of our board of governors, the Rev. William Plomer, and we are all, I am sure, very sorry that illness at the last moment should have prevented him from being here today. But, if I may borrow a familiar metaphor from the – if I may employ a homely metaphor familiar to you all – what we lose on the swings we gain on the roundabouts.'

He paused, and beamed rather freely, to show that this was comedy. I could have told the man it was no use. Not a ripple. The corn chandler leaned against me and muttered 'Whoddidesay?' but that was all.

It's always a nasty jar to wait for the laugh and find that the gag hasn't got across. The bearded bloke was visibly discomposed. At that, however, I think he would have got by, had he not, at this juncture, unfortunately stirred Gussie up again.

'In other words, though deprived of Mr. Plomer, we have with us this afternoon Mr. Fink-Nottle. I am sure that Mr. Fink-Nottle's name is one that needs no introduction to you. It is, I venture to assert, a name that is familiar to us all.'

'Not to you,' said Gussie.

And the next moment I saw what Jeeves had meant when he had described him as laughing heartily. 'Heartily' was absolutely the *mot juste*. It sounded like a gas explosion.

'You didn't seem to know it so dashed well, what, what?' said Gussie. And, reminded apparently by the word 'what' of the word 'Wattle', he repeated the latter some sixteen times with a rising inflection.

'Wattle, Wattle, Wattle,' he concluded. 'Right-ho. Push on.'

But the bearded bloke had shot his bolt. He stood there, licked at last; and, watching him closely, I could see that he was now at the crossroads. I could spot what he was thinking as clearly as if he had confided it to my personal ear. He wanted to sit down and call it a day, I mean, but the thought that gave him pause was that, if he did, he must then either uncork Gussie or take the Fink-Nottle speech as read and get straight on to the actual prize-giving.

It was a dashed tricky thing, of course, to have to decide on the spur of the moment. I was reading in the paper the other day about those birds who are trying to split the atom, the nub being that they haven't the foggiest as to what will happen if they do. It may be all right. On the other hand, it may not be all right. And pretty silly a chap would feel, no doubt, if, having split the atom, he suddenly found the house going up in smoke and himself torn limb from limb.

So with the bearded bloke. Whether he was abreast of the inside facts in Gussie's case, I don't know, but it was obvious to him by this time that he had run into something pretty hot. Trial gallops had shown that

Gussie had his own way of doing things. Those interruptions had been enough to prove to the perspicacious that here, seated on the platform at the big binge of the season, was one who, if pushed forward to make a speech, might let himself go in a rather epoch-making manner.

On the other hand, chain him up and put a green-baize cloth over him, and where were you? The proceeding would be over about half an hour too soon.

It was, as I say, a difficult problem to have to solve, and, left to himself, I don't know what conclusion he would have come to. Personally, I think he would have played it safe. As it happened, however, the thing was taken out of his hands, for at this moment, Gussie, having stretched his arms and yawned a bit, switched on that pebble-beached smile again and tacked down to the edge of the platform.

'Speech,' he said affably.

He then stood with his thumbs in the armholes of his waistcoat, waiting for the applause to die down.

It was some time before this happened, for he had got a very fine hand indeed. I suppose it wasn't often that the boys of Market Snodsbury Grammar School came across a man public-spirited enough to call their head master a silly ass, and they showed their appreciation in no uncertain manner. Gussie may have been one over the eight, but as far as the majority of those present were concerned he was sitting on top of the world.

'Boys,' said Gussie, 'I mean ladies and gentlemen and boys, I do not detain you long, but I suppose on this occasion to feel compelled to say a few auspicious words; Ladies – and boys and gentlemen – we have all listened with interest to the remarks of our friend here who forgot to shave this morning – I don't know his name, but then he didn't know mine – Fitz-Wattle, I mean, absolutely absurd – which squares things up a bit – and we are all sorry that the Reverend What-ever-he-was-called should be dying of adenoids, but after all, here today, gone tomorrow, and all flesh is as grass, and what not, but that wasn't what I wanted to say.

'What I wanted to say was this – and I say it confidently – without fear of contradiction – I say, in short, I am happy to be here on this auspicious occasion and I take much pleasure in kindly awarding the prizes, consisting of the handsome books you see laid out on that table. As Shakespeare says, there are sermons in books, stones in the running brooks, or, rather, the other way about, and there you have it in a nutshell.'

It went well, and I wasn't surprised. I couldn't quite follow some of it, but anybody could see that it was real ripe stuff, and I was amazed that even the course of treatment he had been taking could have rendered so normally tongue-tied a dumb brick as Gussie capable of it.

It just shows, what any member of Parliament will tell you, that if you want real oratory, the preliminary noggin is essential. Unless pie-eyed, you cannot hope to grip.

'Gentlemen,' said Gussie, 'I mean ladies and gentle-men and, of course, boys, what a beautiful world this is. A beautiful world, full of happiness on every side. Let me tell you a little story. Two Irishmen, Pat and Mike, were walking along Broadway, and one said to the other, "Begorrah, the race is not always to the swift," and the other replied, "Faith and begob, education is a drawing out, not a putting in."'

I must say it seemed to me the rottenest story I had ever heard, and I was surprised that Jeeves should have considered it worth shoving into a speech. However, when I taxed him with this later, he said that Gussie had altered the plot a good deal, and I dare say that accounts for it.

At any rate, that was the *conte* as Gussie told it, and when I say that it got a very fair laugh, you will under-stand what a popular favourite he had become with the multitude. There might be a bearded bloke or so on the platform and a small section in the second row who were wishing the speaker would conclude his remarks and resume his seat, but the audience as a whole was for him solidly.

There was applause, and a voice cried: 'Hear, hear!'

'Yes,' said Gussie, 'it is a beautiful world. The sky is blue, the birds are singing, there is optimism everywhere. And why not, boys and ladies and gentlemen? I'm happy, you're happy, we're all happy, even the meanest Irishman that walks along Broadway. Though, as I say, there were two of them – Pat and Mike, one drawing out, the other putting in. I should like you boys, taking the time from me, to give three cheers for this beautiful world. All together now.'

Presently the dust settled down and the plaster stopped falling from the ceiling, and he went on.

'People who say it isn't a beautiful world don't know what they are talking about. Driving here in the car today to award the kind prizes, I was reluctantly compelled to tick off my host on this very point. Old Tom Travers. You will see him sitting there in the second row next to the large lady in beige.'

He pointed helpfully, and the hundred or so Market Snodsburyians who craned their necks in the direction indicated were able to observe Uncle Tom blushing prettily.

'I ticked him off properly, the poor fish. He expressed the opinion that the world was in a deplorable state. I said, "Don't talk rot, old Tom Travers." "I am not accustomed to talk rot," he said. "Then, for a beginner," I said, "you do it dashed well." And I think you will admit, boys and ladies and gentlemen, that that was telling him.'

The audience seemed to agree with him. The point went big. The voice that had said, 'Hear, hear' said 'Hear, hear' again, and my corn chandler hammered the floor vigorously with a large-size walking stick.

'Well, boys,' resumed Gussie, having shot his cuffs and smirked horribly, 'this is the end of the summer term, and many of you, no doubt, are leaving the school. And I don't blame you, because there's a frost in here you could cut with a knife. You are going out into the great world. Soon many of you will be walking along Broadway. And what I want to impress upon you is that, however much you may suffer from adenoids, you must all use every effort to prevent yourselves becoming pessimists and talking rot like old Tom Travers. There in the second row. The fellow with a face rather like a walnut.'

He paused to allow those wishing to do so to refresh themselves with another look at Uncle Tom, and I found myself musing in some little perplexity. Long association with the members of the Drones has put me pretty well in touch with the various ways in which an overdose of the blushful Hippocrene can take the individual, but I had never seen anyone react quite as Gussie was doing.

There was a snap about his work which I had never witnessed before, even in Barmy Fotheringay-Phipps on New Year's Eve.

Jeeves, when I discussed the matter with him later, said it was something to do with inhibitions, if I caught the word correctly, and the suppression of, I think he said, the ego. What he meant, I gathered, was that, owing to the fact that Gussie had just completed a five years' stretch of blameless seclusion among the newts, all the goofiness which ought to have been spread out thin over those five years and had been bottled up during that period came to the surface on this occasion in a lump – or, if you prefer to put it that way, like a tidal wave.

There may be something in this. Jeeves generally knows.

Anyway, be that as it may, I was dashed glad I had had the shrewdness to keep out of that second row. It might be unworthy of the prestige of a Wooster to squash in among the proletariat in the standing-room-only section, but at least, I felt, I was out of the danger zone. So thoroughly had Gussie got it up his nose by now that it seemed to me that had he sighted me he might have become personal about even an old school friend.

'If there's one thing in the world I can't stand,' proceeded Gussie, 'it's a pessimist. Be optimists, boys. You all know the difference between an optimist and a pessimist. An optimist is a man who – well, take the case of two Irishmen walking along Broadway. One is an optimist and one is a pessimist, just as one's name is Pat and the other's Mike ... Why, hullo, Bertie; I didn't know you were here.'

Too late, I endeavoured to go to earth behind the chandler, only to discover that there was no chandler there. Some appointment, suddenly remembered – possibly a promise to his wife that he would be home to tea – had caused him to ooze away while my attention was elsewhere, leaving me right out in the open.

Between me and Gussie, who was now pointing in an offensive manner, there was nothing but a sea of interested faces looking up at me.

'Now, there,' boomed Gussie, continuing to point, 'is an instance of what I mean. Boys and ladies and gentlemen, take a good look at that object standing up there at the back – morning coat, trousers as worn, quiet grey tie, and carnation in buttonhole – you can't miss him. Bertie Wooster, that is, and as foul a pessimist as ever bit a tiger. I tell you I despise that man. And why do I despise him? Because, boys and ladies and gentlemen, he is a pessimist. His attitude is defeatist. When I told him I was going to address you this afternoon, he tried to dissuade me. And do you know why he tried to dissuade me? Because he said my trousers would split up the back.'

The cheers that greeted this were the loudest yet. Anything about splitting trousers went straight to the simple hearts of the young scholars of Market Snodsbury Grammar School. Two in the row in front of me turned purple, and a small lad with freckles seated beside them asked me for my autograph.

'Let me tell you a story about Bertie Wooster.'

A Wooster can stand a good deal, but he cannot stand having his name bandied in a public place. Picking my feet up softly, I was in the very process of executing a quiet sneak for the door, when I perceived that the bearded bloke had at last decided to apply the closure.

Why he hadn't done so before is beyond me. Spell-bound, I take it. And, of course, when a chap is going like a breeze with the public, as Gussie had been, it's not so dashed easy to chip in. However, the prospect of hearing another of Gussie's anecdotes seemed to have done the trick. Rising rather as I had risen from my bench at the beginning of that painful scene with Tuppy in the twilight, he made a leap for the table, snatched up a book and came bearing down on the speaker.

He touched Gussie on the arm, and Gussie, turning sharply and seeing a large bloke with a beard apparently about to bean him with a book, sprang back in an attitude of self-defence.

'Perhaps, as time is getting on, Mr. Fink-Nottle, we had better—'

'Oh, ah,' said Gussie, getting the trend. He relaxed. 'The prizes, eh? Of course, yes. Right-ho. Yes, might as well be shoving along with it. What's this one?'

'Spelling and dictation – P. K. Purvis,' announced the bearded bloke.

'Spelling and dictation – P. K. Purvis,' echoed Gussie, as if he were calling coals. 'Forward, P. K. Purvis.'

Now that the whistle had been blown on his speech, it seemed to me that there was no longer any need for the strategic retreat which I had been planning. I had no wish to tear myself away unless I had to. I mean, I had told Jeeves that this binge would be fraught with interest, and it was fraught with interest. There was a fascination about Gussie's methods which gripped and made one reluctant to pass the thing up provided personal innuendoes were steered clear of. I decided, accordingly, to remain, and presently there was a musical squeaking and P. K. Purvis climbed the platform.

The spelling-and-dictation champ was about three foot six in his squeaking shoes, with a pink face and sandy hair. Gussie patted his hair. He seemed to have taken an immediate fancy to the lad.

'You P. K. Purvis?'

'Sir, yes, sir.'

'It's a beautiful world, P. K. Purvis.'

'Sir, yes, sir.'

'Ah, you've noticed it, have you? Good. You married, by any chance?'

'Sir, no, sir.'

'Get married, P. K. Purvis,' said Gussie earnestly. 'It's the only life . . . Well, here's your book. Looks rather bilge to me from a glance at the title page, but, such as it is, here you are.'

P. K. Purvis squeaked off amidst sporadic applause, but one could not fail to note that the sporadic was followed by a rather strained silence. It was evident that Gussie was striking something of a new note in Market Snodsbury scholastic circles. Looks were exchanged between parent and parent. The bearded bloke had the air of one who has drained the bitter cup. As for Aunt

Dahlia, her demeanour now told only too clearly that her last doubts had been resolved and her verdict was in. I saw her whisper to the Bassett, who sat on her right, and the Bassett nodded sadly and looked like a fairy about to shed a tear and add another star to the Milky Way.

Gussie, after the departure of P. K. Purvis, had fallen into a sort of daydream and was standing with his mouth open and his hands in his pockets. Becoming abruptly aware that a fat kid in knickerbockers was at his elbow, he started violently.

'Hullo!' he said, visibly shaken. 'Who are you?'

'This,' said the bearded bloke, 'is R.V. Smethurst.'

'What's he doing here?' asked Gussie suspiciously.

'You are presenting him with the drawing prize, Mr. Fink-Nottle.'

This apparently struck Gussie as a reasonable explanation. His face cleared.

'That's right, too,' he said ... 'Well, here it is, cocky. You off?' he said, as the kid prepared to withdraw.

'Sir, yes, sir.'

'Wait, R.V. Smethurst. Not so fast. Before you go, there is a question I wish to ask you.'

But the bearded bloke's aim now seemed to be to rush the ceremonies a bit. He hustled R.V. Smethurst off stage rather like a chucker-out in a pub regretfully ejecting an old and respected customer, and starting paging G.G. Simmons. A moment later the latter was up and coming, and conceive my emotion when it was announced that the subject on which he had clicked was Scripture knowledge. One of us, I mean to say.

G.G. Simmons was an unpleasant, perky-looking stripling, mostly front teeth and spectacles, but I gave him a big hand. We Scripture-knowledge sharks stick together.

Gussie, I was sorry to see, didn't like him. There was in his manner, as he regarded G.G. Simmons, none of the chumminess which had marked it during his interview with P. K. Purvis or, in a somewhat lesser degree, with R.V. Smethurst. He was cold and distant.

'Well, G.G. Simmons.'

'Sir, yes, sir.'

'What do you mean – sir, yes, sir? Dashed silly thing to say. So you've won the Scripture-knowledge prize, have you?'

'Sir, yes, sir.'

'Yes,' said Gussie, 'you look just the sort of little tick who would. And yet,' he said, pausing and eyeing the child keenly, 'how are we to know that this has all been open and above board? Let me test you, G.G. Simmons. What was What's-His-Name – the chap who begat Thingummy? Can you answer me that, Simmons?'

'Sir, no, sir.'

Gussie turned to the bearded bloke.

'Fishy,' he said. 'Very fishy. This boy appears to be totally lacking in Scripture knowledge.'

The bearded bloke passed a hand across his forehead.

'I can assure you, Mr. Fink-Nottle, that every care was taken to ensure a correct marking and that Simmons outdistanced his competitors by a wide margin.'

'Well, if you say so,' said Gussie doubtfully. 'All right, G.G. Simmons, take your prize.'

'Sir, thank you, sir.'

'But let me tell you that there's nothing to stick on side about in winning a prize for Scripture knowledge. Bertie Wooster—'

I don't know when I've had a nastier shock. I had been going on the assumption that, now that they had stopped him making his speech, Gussie's fangs had been drawn, as you might say. To duck my head down and resume my edging toward the door was with me the work of a moment.

'Bertie Wooster won the Scripture-knowledge prize at a kids' school we were at together, and you know what he's like. But, of course, Bertie frankly cheated. He succeeded in scrounging that Scripture-knowledge trophy over the heads of better men by means of some of the rawest and most brazen swindling methods ever witnessed even at a school where such things were common. If that man's pockets, as he entered the examination-room, were not stuffed to bursting-point with lists of the kings of Judah—'

I heard no more. A moment later I was out in God's

air, fumbling with a fevered foot at the self-starter of the old car.

The engine raced. The clutch slid into position. I tooted and drove off.

My ganglions were still vibrating as I ran the car into the stables of Brinkley Court, and it was a much shaken Bertram who tottered up to his room to change into something loose. Having donned flannels, I lay down on the bed for a bit, and I suppose I must have dozed off, for the next thing I remember is finding Jeeves at my side.

I sat up. 'My tea, Jeeves?'

'No, sir. It is nearly dinner-time.'

The mists cleared away.

'I must have been asleep.'

'Yes, sir.'

'Nature taking its toll of the exhausted frame.'

'Yes, sir.'

'And enough to make it.'

'Yes, sir.'

'And now it's nearly dinner-time, you say? All right. I am in no mood for dinner, but I suppose you had better lay out the clothes.'

'It will not be necessary, sir. The company will not be dressing tonight. A cold collation has been set out in the dining-room.'

'Why's that?'

'It was Mrs. Travers's wish that this should be done in order to minimize the work for the staff, who are attending a dance at Sir Percival Stretchley-Budd's residence tonight.'

'Of course, yes. I remember. My Cousin Angela told me. Tonight's the night, what? You going, Jeeves?'

'No, sir. I am not very fond of this form of entertainment in the rural districts, sir.'

'I know what you mean. These country binges are all the same. A piano, one fiddle, and a floor like sandpaper. Is Anatole going? Angela hinted not.'

'Miss Angela was correct, sir. Monsieur Anatole is in bed.'

'Temperamental blighters, these Frenchmen.'

'Yes, sir.'

There was a pause.

'Well, Jeeves,' I said, 'it was certainly one of those afternoons, what?'

'Yes, sir.'

'I cannot recall one more packed with incident. And I left before the finish.'

'Yes, sir. I observed your departure.'

'You couldn't blame me for withdrawing.'

'No, sir. Mr. Fink-Nottle had undoubtedly become embarrassingly personal.'

'Was there much more of it after I went?'

'No, sir. The proceedings terminated very shortly.

Mr. Fink-Nottle's remarks with reference to Master G.G. Simmons brought about an early closure.'

'But he had finished his remarks about G.G. Simmons.'

'Only temporarily, sir. He resumed them immediately after your departure. If you recollect, sir, he had already proclaimed himself suspicious of Master Simmons's bona fides, and he now proceeded to deliver a violent verbal attack upon the young gentleman, asserting that it was impossible for him to have won the Scripture-knowledge prize without systematic cheating on an impressive scale. He went so far as to suggest that Master Simmons was well known to the police.'

'Golly, Jeeves!'

'Yes, sir. The words did create a considerable sensation. The reaction of those present to this accusation I should describe as mixed. The young students appeared pleased and applauded vigorously, but Master Simmons's mother rose from her seat and addressed Mr. Fink-Nottle in terms of strong protest.'

'Did Gussie seem taken aback? Did he recede from his position?'

'No, sir. He said that he could see it all now, and hinted at a guilty liaison between Master Simmons's mother and the head master, accusing the latter of having cooked the marks, as his expression was, in order to gain favour with the former.'

'You don't mean that?'

'Yes, sir.'

'Egad, Jeeves! And then—'

'They sang the national anthem, sir.'

'Surely not?'

'Yes, sir.'

'At a moment like that?'

'Yes, sir.'

'Well, you were there and you know, of course, but I should have thought the last thing Gussie and this woman would have done in the circs would have been to start singing duets.'

'You misunderstand me, sir. It was the entire company who sang. The head master turned to the organist and said something to him in a low tone. Upon which the latter began to play the national anthem, and the proceedings terminated.'

'I see. About time, too.'

'Yes, sir. Mrs. Simmons's attitude had become unquestionably menacing.'

I pondered. What I had heard was, of course, of a nature to excite pity and terror, not to mention alarm and despondency, and it would be paltering with the truth to say that I was pleased about it. On the other hand, it was all over now, and it seemed to me that the thing to do was not to mourn over the past but to fix the mind on the bright future. I mean to say, Gussie might have lowered the existing Worcestershire record for goofiness and definitely forfeited all chance of becoming Market Snodsbury's favourite son, but you couldn't get away from the fact that he had proposed to Madeline Bassett, and you had to admit that she had accepted him.

I put this to Jeeves.

'A frightful exhibition,' I said, 'and one which will very possibly ring down history's pages. But we must not forget, Jeeves, that Gussie, though now doubtless looked upon in the neighbourhood as the world's worst freak, is all right otherwise.'

'No, sir.'

I did not get quite this.

'When you say "No, sir", do you mean "Yes, sir"?'

'No, sir. I mean "No, sir."'

'He is not all right otherwise?'

'No, sir.'

'But he's betrothed.'

'No longer, sir. Miss Bassett has severed the engagement.'

'You don't mean that?'

'Yes, sir.'

I wonder if you have noticed a rather peculiar thing about this chronicle. I allude to the fact that at one time or another practically everybody playing a part in it has had occasion to bury his or her face in his or her hands. I have participated in some pretty glutinous affairs in my time, but I think that never before or since have I been mixed up with such a solid body of brow clutchers.

Uncle Tom did it, if you remember. So did Gussie. So did Tuppy. So, probably, though I have no data, did Anatole, and I wouldn't put it past the Bassett. And Aunt Dahlia, I have no doubt, would have done it, too, but for the risk of disarranging the carefully fixed coiffure.

Well, what I am trying to say is that at this juncture I did it myself. Up went the hands and down went the head, and in another jiffy I was clutching as energetically as the best of them . . .

CONCLUSION:
'MY BATTLE WITH DRINK'

Wodehouse wrote this comic piece in 1915 in his capacity as an occa-
sional contributor to Vanity Fair *magazine, who billed it as the first*
in a series of 'Great Redemption Stories . . . Confided by the Addict
to P.G. Wodehouse'. The manner in which the tale's narrator, Cyril,
finds his way onto the straight and narrow is one to which all of us,
surely, can raise a glass. In addition, contemporary readers might
like to know that Riker and Hegeman was a then-popular chain of
American drugstores where patrons could treat themselves to such
dairy-based beverages as bulgarzoon, zoolak and kumyss. 'How
perfectly foul', as Bertie Wooster would say.

I could tell my story in two words – the two words 'I
drank'. (But while editors make a practice of paying
for human documents by length, I'm hanged if I'm
going to do so.) But I was not always a drinker. This is
the story of my downfall – and of my rise, for, through
the influence of a good woman, I have, thank Heaven,
risen from the depths and can now go through Times

Square without even hesitating at the drug-store. The other day I met a wild young fellow, a chum of my unregenerate days, up in New York for a good time. He took my arm and began to steer me to the nearest Riker and Hegeman. 'Come, Cyril,' he cried. 'We shall only be young once. Let us enjoy life while we may. I'll blow you to a nut sundae.' I shook him off. 'No, Clarence,' I replied, kindly but firmly, 'I am through with all that sort of thing. I am saved.'

I lost a friend, but I retained my self-respect.

I was not always a slave of the soda-fountain. The thing stole upon me gradually, as it does upon so many young men. As a boy, I remember taking a glass of root-beer, but it did not grip me then. I can recall that I even disliked the taste. I was a young man before temptation really came upon me. My downfall began when I joined the Yonkers Short-Hand and Typewriting Correspondence College.

It was then that I first made acquaintance with the awful power of ridicule. They were a hard-living set at college – reckless youths. They frequented movie-palaces. They thought nothing of winding up an evening with a couple of egg-phosphates and a chocolate fudge. They laughed at me when I refused to join them. I was only twenty. My character was undeveloped. I could not endure their scorn. The next time I was offered a drink I accepted. They were pleased, I remember. They called me 'Good old Cyril!' and a good sport and other complimentary names. I was intoxicated with sudden popularity.

How vividly I can recall that day! The shining counter, the placards advertising strange mixtures with ice-cream as their basis, the busy men behind the counter, the half cynical, half pitying eyes of the girl in the cage where you bought the soda-checks. She had seen so many happy, healthy boys through that little hole in the wire netting, so many thoughtless boys all eagerness for their first soda, clamouring to set their foot on the primrose path that leads to destruction.

It was an apple marshmallow sundae, I recollect. I dug my spoon into it with an assumption of gaiety which I was far from feeling. The first mouthful almost nauseated me. It was like cold hair-oil. But I stuck to it. I could not back out now. I could not bear to forfeit the newly-won esteem of my comrades. They were gulping their sundaes down with the speed and enjoyment of old hands. I set my teeth, and persevered, and by degrees a strange exhilaration began to steal over me. I felt that I had burnt my boats and bridges; that I had crossed the Rubicon. I was reckless. I ordered another round. I accosted perfect strangers and forced sundaes upon them. I was the life and soul of that wild party.

The next morning brought remorse. I did not feel well. I had pains, physical and mental. But I could not go back now. I was too weak to dispense with my popularity. I was only a boy, and on the previous evening the captain of the Checkers Club, to whom I looked up with an almost worshipping reverence, had slapped me on the back and told me that I was a corker. I felt that nothing could be excessive payment for such an honour. That night I gave a party at which orange phosphate flowed like water. It was the turning-point.

I had got the habit!

I will pass briefly over the next few years. I continued to sink deeper and deeper into the slough. I knew all the drug-store clerks in New York by their first names, and they called me by mine. I no longer even had to specify the abomination I desired. I simply handed the man my ten-cent check and said: 'The usual, Jimmy,' and he understood. I neglected my business and undermined my health. It became a regular thing for me to steal out during office hours and hurry to a drug-store. My manner with customers became strange. I was nervous and *distrait*. I became a secret candy-eater.

At first, considerations of health did not trouble me. I was young and strong, and my constitution quickly threw off the effects of my dissipation. Then, gradually, I began to feel worse. I was losing my grip. I found a difficulty in concentrating my attention on my work. I had dizzy spells. Eventually I went to a doctor. He examined me thoroughly, and shook his head.

'If I am to do you any good,' he said, 'you must tell me all. You must hold no secrets from me.'

'Doctor,' I said, covering my face with my hands, 'I am a confirmed soda-fiend.'

He gave me a long lecture and a longer list of instructions. I must take air and exercise and I must become a total abstainer from sundaes of all descriptions. I must avoid limeade like the plague, and if anybody offered me a Bulgarzoon I was to knock him down and shout for the nearest policeman.

I learned then for the first time what a bitterly hard thing it is for a man in a large and wicked city to keep away from soda when once he has got the habit. Everything was against me. The old convivial circle began to shun me. I could not join in their revels and they began to look on me as a grouch. In the end I fell, and in one wild orgy undid all the good of a month's abstinence. I was desperate then. I felt that nothing could save me, and I might as well give up the struggle. I drank two pinap-o-lades, three grapefruitolas and an egg-zoolak, before pausing to take breath.

And then, one day, I luckily met May, the girl who effected my reformation. She was a clergyman's daughter who, to support her widowed mother, had accepted a non-speaking part in a musical comedy production entitled 'Oh Joy! Oh Pep!' Our acquaintance ripened, and one night I asked her out to supper.

I look on that moment as the happiest of my life. I met her at the stage-door, and conducted her to the nearest soda-fountain. We were inside and I was buying the checks before she realized where she was, and I shall never forget her look of mingled pain and horror.

'And I thought you were a live one!' she murmured.

I confessed everything to her. It seemed that she had been looking forward to a little lobster and champagne. The idea was absolutely new to me. She quickly convinced me, however, that such was the only refreshment which she would consider, and she recoiled with unconcealed aversion from my suggestion of a Kumyss and an Eva Tanguay. That night I tasted wine for the first time, and my reformation began.

It was hard at first, desperately hard. Something inside me was trying to pull me back to the sundaes for which I craved, but I resisted the impulse. Always with her divinely sympathetic encouragement, I gradually acquired a taste for alcohol. And suddenly, one evening, like a flash it came upon me that I had shaken off the cursed yoke that held me down; that I never wanted to see the inside of a drug-store again. Cocktails, at first repellent, have at last become palatable to me. I drink high-balls for breakfast. I am saved.

FURTHER READING

The following Wodehouse titles are extracted in this volume, and all are available from Arrow, an imprint of Penguin Random House and Everyman's Library.

Barmy in Wonderland

In this powerful love story, Cyril Fotheringay-Phipps invests his wealth in a stage production, driven by his love for Miss Dinty Moore.

Full Moon

When the moon is full at Blandings, strange things happen including a renowned painter being miraculously revivified to paint a portrait of the beloved pig The Empress of Blandings, decades after his death . . .

Jeeves in the Offing

When Jeeves goes on holiday to Herne Bay, Bertie's life collapses; finding his mysterious engagement announced in *The Times* and encountering his nemesis Sir Roderick Glossop in disguise, Bertie hightails it to Herne Bay. Then the fun really starts ...

Jeeves Takes Charge

This collection of stories follows Bertie Wooster at risk of being forced into a marriage he is not keen on, looking after Aunt Agatha's disappearing dog, and taking romance into his own hands by playing Cupid to a pair of middle-aged lovers.

Jill the Reckless

Chorus girl Jill Mariner has not had the best of luck in life – in financial ruins and with a broken engagement she is nevertheless determined to find true love.

Carry on, Jeeves

In his new role as valet to Bertie Wooster, Jeeve's first duty is to create a miracle hangover cure. From that moment, the partnership that is Jeeves and Wooster never looks back ...

Cocktail Time

Frederick, Earl of Ickenham, remains young at heart. So his jape of using a catapult to ping the silk top hat off his grumpy half-brother-in-law is nothing out of the ordinary but the consequences abound with possibilities.

The Code of the Woosters

Purloining an antique cow creamer under the instruction of

the indomitable Aunt Dahlia is the least of Bertie's tasks, for he has to play Cupid while feuding with Spode.

Big Money

Berry Conway, employee of dyspeptic American millionaire Torquil Patterson Frisby, has inherited a large number of shares in the Dream Come True copper mine. Of course they're worthless . . . aren't they?

A Damsel in Distress

The Earl of Marshmoreton just wants a quiet life pottering around his garden, supported by his portly butler Keggs. However when his spirited daughter Lady Maud is placed under house-arrest due to an unfortunate infatuation, and American George Bevan determines to claim her heart, the Earl is allowed no such reprieve . . .

Doctor Sally

Bill Bannister's world is turned upside down when he meets the delectable Dr. Sally Smith. Love is in the air; however the arrival of Lottie Higginbotham, with whom Bill is already involved, complicates matters. Will Bill Bannister and Dr. Sally Smith get their happy ending?

Eggs, Beans and Crumpets

This assortment of delightfully humorous stories feature a range of Wodehouse's most outrageous characters, including newly-weds Rosie M. Banks and Bingo.

The Girl in Blue

Young Jerry West has a few problems, including uncles with butlers who aren't all they seem, and a love for the woman he is not due to marry ... When his uncle's miniature Gainsborough, *The Girl in Blue*, is stolen, Jerry sets out on a mission to find her ... Will everything come right in the process?

Heavy Weather

After being told his memoir will no longer be published, Lord Tilbury travels to Blandings Castle in order to steal a document. However, Sir Gregory Parsloe-Parsloe and Lady Constance Keeble are also in search of this file in order to avert the marriage of Ronnie Fish and Sue Brown.

Hot Water

In the heady atmosphere of a 1930s French Château, J Wellington Gedge only wants to return to his life in California, where everything is at it seems ...

Indiscretions of Archie

This book portrays the trials and tribulations of Archibald "Archie" Moffam, in particular his attempts to win the approval of his millionaire father-in-law Daniel Brewster.

The Inimitable, Jeeves

In pages stalked by the carnivorous Aunt Agatha, Bingo Little embarks on a relationship rollercoaster and Bertie needs Jeeves' help to narrowly evade the clutches of terrifying Honoria Glossop ...

Jeeves and the Feudal Spirit

A moustachioed Bertie must live up to 'Stilton' Cheesewright's expectations in the Drones Club darts tournament, or risk being beaten to a pulp by 'Stilton', jealous of his fiancée Florence's affections ...

Joy in the Morning

Trapped in rural Steeple Bumpleigh with old flame Florence Craye, her new and suspicious fiancée Stilton Cheesewright, and two-faced Edwin the Boy Scout, Bertie desperately needs Jeeves to save him ...

Laughing Gas

Joey Cooley, golden-curled Hollywood child film star, and Reginald, six-foot tall boxer Earl of Havershot, are both under anaesthetic in the dentist's when their identities are swapped in the fourth dimension.

The Man with Two Left Feet

This fascinating assortment of stories focuses on relationships, sports and household pets. Interestingly, these stories do not follow any of Wodehouse's regular well-known characters; however, "Extricating Young Gussie" is renowned for the first appearance of some of Wodehouse's most popular and loved characters, Jeeves and his master, Bertie Wooster.

The Mating Season

In an idyllic Tudor manor in a picture-perfect English village, Bertie is in disguise as Gussie Fink-Nottle, Gussie is in disguise as Bertram Wooster and Jeeves, also in disguise, is the only one who can set things right . . .

Meet Mr Mulliner

Sitting in the Angler's Rest, drinking hot scotch and lemon, Mr Mulliner has fabulous stories to tell of the extraordinary behaviour of his far flung family. This includes Wilfred, whose formula for Buck-U-Uppo enables elephants to face tigers with the necessary nonchalance.

Mr Mulliner Speaking

Holding court in the bar-parlour of the Angler's Rest, Mr Mulliner reveals what happened to The Man Who Gave Up Smoking, what the Something Squishy was that the butler had on a silver salver, and what caused the dreadful Unpleasantness at Bludleigh Court.

My Man Jeeves

This series includes eight short stories in the collection; half of which feature the beloved characters Jeeves and his master Bertie Wooster, while the others follow Reggie Pepper, an early prototype for Wooster.

Nothing Serious

These stories see the return of old friends from the Drones Club including Bingo Little and Mrs Bingo, Freddie Widgeon, Agnes Flack and Horace Bewstridge.

Pigs Have Wings

Can the Empress of Blandings avoid a pignapping to win the Fat Pigs class at the Shropshire Show for the third year running?

Right Ho, Jeeves

Bertie assumes his alter-ego of Cupid and arranges the engagement of Gussie Fink-Nottle to Tuppy Glossop. Thankfully, Jeeves is ever present to correct the blundering plans hatched by his master.

Service with a Smile

When Clarence, Ninth Earl of Emsworth, must travel to London for the opening of Parliament, he grudgingly leaves beloved pig, the Empress of Blandings, at home. When he returns, he must call upon Uncle Fred to restore normality to the chaos instilled during his absence . . .

Spring Fever

With an indecent reputation, Jimmy Crocker sets out to win back the love of his life while Lord Dawlish plans to make his fortune beginning with an adventure in America.

Summer Lightning

The Empress of Blandings – the prize-winning pig and all-consuming passion of Clarence, Ninth Earl of Emsworth—has disappeared. Suspects within the Castle abound ... Did the butler do it?

Ukridge

Money makes the world go round for Stanley Featherstone-haugh Ukridge – looking like an animated blob of mustard in his bright yellow raincoat – and when there isn't enough of it, the world just has to spin a bit faster.

Uncle Dynamite

Meet Frederick Altamount Cornwallis Twistleton, Fifth Earl of Ickenham. Better known as Uncle Fred, an old boy of such a sunny and youthful nature that explosions of sweetness and light detonate all around him.

Uncle Fred in the Springtime

Uncle Fred believes he can achieve anything in the springtime; however, disguised as a loonydoctor and trying to prevent prize pig, the Empress of Blandings, from falling into the hands of the unscrupulous Duke of Dunstable, he is stretched to his limit ...

Young Men in Spats

Meet the Young Men in Spats – all innocent members of the Drones Club, all hopeless suitors, and all busy betting their sometimes non-existent fortunes on highly improbable outcomes. That is when they're not recovering from driving their sports cars *through* Marble Arch ...

A Few Quick Ones

A collection of short stories featuring the inhabitants of the Drones Club and the reappearance of old friends including Mr. Mulliner, Ukridge, Freddie Widgeon, Bingo Little and Bertie Wooster and Jeeves.

Frozen Assets

In hope of receiving his godfather's legacy, Edmund Biffen Christopher must avoid being arrested. However, Lord Tilbury sets out to hasten Biffen's fall in the hope that he may inherit the legacy instead.